Jonathan Swift

Unpublished Letters of Dean Swift

Jonathan Swift

Unpublished Letters of Dean Swift

ISBN/EAN: 9783744714242

Printed in Europe, USA, Canada, Australia, Japan

Cover: Foto ©Thomas Meinert / pixelio.de

More available books at **www.hansebooks.com**

Unpublished Letters
of
Dean Swift

Unpublished Letters

of

Dean Swift

EDITED BY

GEORGE BIRKBECK HILL, D.C.L., LL.D

HON. FELLOW OF PEMBROKE COLLEGE, OXFORD

ILLUSTRATED

London

T. FISHER UNWIN

PATERNOSTER SQUARE

1899

PREFACE

I DESIRE to express my acknowledgments for assistance received in editing these Letters to the Rev. E. M. Walker, Fellow of Queen's College, Oxford, to Mr. C. E. Doble, M.A., of the Clarendon Press, to Professor Dowden, to Mr. J. J. Digges La Touche, LL.D., Keeper of the Dublin State Paper Office, and to the Rev. William Reynell. Above all, I am indebted to Mr. G. K. Fortescue, one of the Assistant Keepers of the British Museum, and to Mr. F. Elrington Ball. To Mr. Ivon H. Price, LL.D., I owe the views of Laracor. Miss Wilmot-Chetwode of Woodbrook I have to thank for the photographs of the portraits of her ancestors, Knightley Chetwode and his wife, and also for one of a view of their house.

TABLE OF CONTENTS

I.

PAGE

The poor Dean of St. Patrick's—A rebellious choir—Not a horse to be had—Idle claims—Noise and bonfires. . 1

II.

The little subaltern cares of life—Important nothings—A great cat and an old woman—Everything as bad as possible—The way traced for the Pretender. 9

III.

Whigs—A housekeeper with a tolerable face not allowed—Public and private hay—A bonfire to save the windows—Forty-six dozen bottles and no wine—Servants . . . 13

IV.

A call at Woodbrook 18

V.

Chetwode's *Advice to a Young Lady* 18

VI.

Full of company—A Tory ballad—Coffee—The Marquis of Wharton 19

VII.

Tories put out of the King's peace—A smart Dean—Mending the public—Servants spoilt—A limitation put on preaching—Endowments of St. Patrick's 22

VIII.

PAGE

Vicars-choral—Ignorance of news   .   28

IX.

Grandmother's proverbs—Shakespeare   30

X.

Letters opened in the Post Office—The Archbishop's protection
—Papers hidden—Play-house riot—The Earl of Oxford
and Viscount Bolingbroke in danger   34

XI.

Duke of Ormond impeached—Talk of sending for Swift—
Remedies for a disordered head—A collegian found guilty
—Informers—Report of the Secret Committee—The old
slander about the Pretender—Bolingbroke's flight   .   .   41

XII.

Snuff—Chetwode's walk—Bishop of London's *Letter to his
Clergy*—Tumults in London—Letter from the Duchess
of Ormond—The Duke of Shrewsbury threatened—Prior
in prison—Earl of Oxford's intrepidity—Tom's locks pulled   49

XIII.

Duke of Ormond's flight—Rumours of an invasion—Tories and
Jacobites—Habeas Corpus Act suspended—Cherry Brandy
—Licence of Absence   59

XIV.

Chetwode at Chester—Irish parliament   65

XV.

Chetwode in London—The Grattans—The Dragon—Horrible
fears of the rebels—Swift's friends—Poor Ben—The Pretender landing—Chetwode's suspicions—Swift expects to be
trusted—Parliament mad—Honest people get into corners   69

XVI.

Chetwode's return from abroad—The change from dukes to
Irish squires and parsons—Jack Grattan and Dan Jackson
—Swift no politician—Two oracles   78

XVII.

PAGE

Spirit above fortune — People of one's own level — Lady
Hamilton 84

XVIII.

Chetwode horribly treated — Oath of abjuration — Titles to
crowns — Improving land 87

XIX.

Chetwode's quarrel with a colonel—Bravery—Archbishop of
Dublin—The Lord-Lieutenant 90

XX.

Chetwode's prosecution—Building—No horses to be had—
Mist's Journal—White roses 93

XXI.

Galstown—Swift not unkind or forgetful—Ill-will of folk in
power—Disputes about meres and bounds—Righteous
disputants 99

XXII.

Charles Jervas—Swift disconcerted and confounded by deafness   104

XXIII.

Gabbling with the French clergy—Death of Dean Pratt—The
Bank kicked out—Liberties of the Deanery—Planting trees
—Plague, poverty, and famine 106

XXIV.

Deafness—Trebles and counter-tenors—A country gentleman
king over his own district—Lime and stone—Preparing for
the plague—Tradesmen breaking. 114

XXV.

A remedy for deafness—Scurvy writings fathered on Swift—An
Act of Parliament about the plague—Disaffected Whigs
—*The Reformer*—Ignorance of news—Servant dying . . 120

XXVI.

PAGE

Chetwode in trouble—Chief Justice Whitshed—Planting trees and draining bogs—Swift sometimes concerned for persons, but for things never 128

XXVII.

Chetwode's prosecution—The Archbishop of Dublin . . . 133

XXVIII.

Chetwode's prosecution—Dangerous times 134

XXIX.

Chetwode's prosecution 136

XXX.

Chetwode's prosecution—Dr. Coghill—Irish parliament—Calmness of friends 136

XXXI.

Chetwode's petition 139

XXXII.

Chetwode's petition 140

XXXIII.

Chetwode's petition—How to move the Secretary of the Lord-Lieutenant 141

XXXIV.

Over head and ears in mortar—Chetwode's prosecution—Death of the Primate, Chief Justice, and Lord Oxford—Mr. Stopford 143

XXXV.

Irish carriers—A *Drapier Letter*. 149

XXXVI.

PAGE

Chetwode's separation from his wife—Mr. Stopford—Discipline
of Oxford University—The noise of seven watermills in
Swift's ears—Perfumed paper   153

XXXVII.

Trinity College, Dublin—Fellow-Commoners and Pensioners—
Verses on Wood—The Grand Jury   159

XXXVIII.

Chetwode's separation from his wife—Proposed allowance—
Lord Cadogan—Swift at the Lord-Lieutenant's *levée* .   . 162

XXXIX.

Mrs. Chetwode's place of residence—*Drapier Letters*—Rumours
of a new Lord-Lieutenant   166

XL.

A wife's debts—Stories of Swift at the *levée*—How to pass the
time   169

XLI.

Quilca—Failing sight—Levelling mountains—A thievish race—
Health and fortune—A cursed wall—Lenders of money—
Land as a security—Young travellers—A reward offered for
the discoverer of the Draper—Dr. Delany   172

XLII.

Bad weather—Inspecting labourers—Reading easy trash—Man
a ridiculous creature   184

XLIII.

A proposed ride .   .   .   .   - 187

XLIV.

Cadenus and Vanessa—Vanessa's executors—The baseness of
mankind—Swift in London—The stir people made with him 189

XLV.

PAGE

Swift's return to Dublin—Stella's illness—Friends in England 198

XLVI.

Monkish way of living—*Gulliver's Travels*—Mangled in the
press—Improvements of land—The deanery garden—
Illness of the Archbishop 202

XLVII.

Swift's second visit to England—Giddiness and deafness—At
Court—Politics in England and Ireland—The public an old
tattered house—Dublin the most disagreeable place in
Europe—Raps of quality 210

XLVIII.

Chetwode's son—Study of Law—The old road of learning . 219

XLIX.

A solitary life—Dinner with the Chapter—Scurrilities—The
republic of fools and knaves—Safety in obscurity . . 220

L.

Want of ready money—Borrowing from the poor-bag—Universal
despair—A law-suit 224

LI.

Death of Mrs. Chetwode—Jackman's failure—Chetwode involved
—How to deal with creditors—Cheap living in England . 230

LII.

Chetwode's proposed second marriage—His money difficulties—
Giving advice—Swift's law-suit 233

LIII.

Archbishop Sheldon—Getting money with a wife . 236

LIV.

Fencing against the evils of age and sickness—Country life in
Ireland—Enemies lost by retirement—Chetwode's informa-
tion of passages in private life—The world—Libels against
Swift 240

LV.

PAGE

Chetwode's attack on Swift—Horace—His Eminence of St. Patrick's—St. Ambrose—Swift in riding costume . . 244

LVI.

Swift's lameness—Wycherley on ceremony in friendship . . 247

LVII.

Chetwode's knowledge of the secrets of families—Dealing with old Nick—His scheme of thinking, conversing, and living —People of title—Swift's friends all middling people— Chetwode's wooing—Swift's ambition cured—Chetwode's Latin and divinity—Letters a standing witness against a man 248

LVIII.

Chetwode's reply—Chief Justice Whitshed—Great names and titles—A riddle for Swift—Logic, Latin, and divinity— Charms of women—Swifts affectation 256

LIST OF ILLUSTRATIONS

Jonathan Swift, from an engraving by P. Fourdrinier of a portrait taken of him in his old
age by Charles Jervas. It was under the
tuition of this painter — "robust and debonair" as Gay describes him—that Pope
put himself in early manhood, "when he had
a strong inclination to unite the art of paint-
ing with that of poetry." In the epistle that
the poet addressed to him he unites their
fate and fame, and hopes that together they
may "shine through long succeeding age."
The painter's brightness soon began to grow
dim. When Sir Joshua was asked by Miss
Reynolds " how it happened that none of
Jervas's pictures were to be seen, he replied :
' Because they are all up in the garret.' "
The date of Fourdrinier's engraving is fixed
by a letter of Thomas Carter, the Master of
the Rolls in Ireland. On March 11, 1735-6,
writing about the print to Swift, he said : " I

have no doubt the printer will have occasion
for a great many cargoes from our friend
Mr. Jervas "   ...   .   *Frontispiece*

Woodbrook, from a sketch taken last century.
It shows the house as Swift knew it.   Great
additions have been made by later owners
                              To face page xx

The Ruins of Laracor Vicarage, from a photograph taken by Dr. Ivon H. Price.   " The
Vicarage," Dr. Price writes, " was a very
large one, and covered a large piece of what
is now a garden on the right-hand side of
the picture.   Unfortunately the ruin has been
coped with mortar to preserve it.   The
photograph was taken from the public road."
" There this fragment of a wall remains,"
wrote a former vicar, " gaunt and solitary,
the most interesting relic of the abode of an
extraordinary man " ...   ...   *To face page* 7

Swift's Well at Laracor, from a photograph by
Dr. Ivon H. Price.   " The well is situated
under the ash-tree in the centre of the picture, and can be reached through the gap in
the road wall.   It is stated that it was in
the cellar of the old Vicarage, and that Swift
used to boast that his cellar never ran dry,
and that he had more liquor in it than many
of his wealthy friends had in theirs.   There
are other cases in the neighbourhood of wells
in wine cellars "   ..   ...   *To face page* 27

Laracor Church, with its present vicar, the Rev. Mr. Conolly, in the foreground, from a photograph by · Dr. Ivon H. Price. Of Swift's church nothing remains, except, as I learn from Dr. Price, "several curiously carved stones in the vestry, which are said to be portions of it." In 1856, when the old building was taken down, as it stood " at the extreme verge of a large parish," a proposal was made that it should be rebuilt in a central position. The Vicar, "moved by the *genius loci*, had the old site maintained, and consequently the new church stands precisely where the Dean's was "

To face page 86

Jonathan Swift, from an engraving by George Vertue of a portrait of him by Charles Jervas, painted in 1708, but retouched two years later. On September 9, 1710, Swift wrote to Stella : "On Monday Jervas is to retouch my picture." Two days later he wrote : " Seven morning. I am rising to go to Jervas to finish my picture, and 'tis shaving day, so good-morrow, M.D. . . . Ten at night. I sat four hours this morning to Jervas, who has given my picture quite another turn, and now approves it entirely ; but we must have the approbation of the town. If I were rich enough, I would get a copy of it, and bring it over." *To face page* 100

The west front of St. Patrick's Cathedral, from
James Malton's Views of Dublin, taken in
1791 ...   ., *To face page* 107

Title-page of the first edition of the first
Drapier Letter.   The first edition is a pamphlet of sixteen pages in small octavo, very
roughly printed on bad paper and with many
errors of the press.   Badly printed as were
most of the Dublin pamphlets of Swift's
time, this Drapier Letter is far below the
average   ...   .   *To face page* 150

Page five of the same edition ...   *To face page* 152

Knightley Chetwode.—This portrait and Mrs.
Chetwode's (page 230), by an unknown
artist, "were," I am told, "apparently done
at the time of their marriage in 1700.   They
are painted on copper, slightly larger than
miniature size"   ...   ...   *To face page* 166

An allegorical picture engraved by Vertue.   In
it Swift is represented as trampling on
William Wood, whose halfpence lie scattered
below him.   On the right Hibernia, with her
harp lying by her, is receiving a Drapier
Letter; on the left a poor woman is scornfully
holding out one of the brazen coins.   Two
cherubs are descending with a laurel leaf to
crown the Dean, who, in his robes, is seated
on a kind of throne between the Temple of
Fame and his own cathedral.   Sir Walter
Scott describes a somewhat similar picture

by Francis Bindon at Howth Castle. In it "the genius of Ireland extends the laurel wreath," while the woman on the left is not there ... ... *To face page* 175

Jonathan Swift, engraved by Vanhaecken from a drawing by Markham after Bindon. Mr. Sidney Colvin informs me that "like almost all the engraved portraits of Swift, this one goes back to the full-length original picture painted by Bindon. The words 'Markham delin.,' which appear on the plate, must mean that Markham was the name (otherwise unknown) of the draughtsman who adapted the picture for the purpose of Vanhaecken's engraving, turning the full-length standing figure into a half-length seated one, adding the chair and altering the background"

To face page 198

Mrs. Chetwode... ... ... *To face page* 230

Stella's Cottage from a photograph by Dr. Ivon H. Price, "It is situated," Dr. Price informs me, "on the roadside between Laracor and Trim, and is about half a mile from Laracor. The doorway is remarkable, and this design is rare in Ireland. It is a roomy, comfortable cottage. The road passes on the right side of the picture past the gable end" ... ... *To face page* 239

WOODBROOK, FROM A SKETCH TAKEN LAST CENTURY.

[To face page xx.

INTRODUCTION

JOHN FORSTER, who lived to complete but one of the three volumes in which he had planned to write the Life of Jonathan Swift, speaks in his preface of his hero's correspondence "with his friend Knightley Chetwode, of Woodbrook, during the seventeen years (1714–1731) which followed his appointment to the deanery of St. Patrick's. Of these letters," Forster goes on to say, " the richest addition to the correspondence of this most masterly of English letter-writers since it was first collected, more does not need to be said here ; but of the late representative of the Chetwode family I crave permission to add a word. His rare talents and taste suffered from his delicate health and fastidious temperament, but in my life I have seen few things more delightful than his pride in the connection of his race and name with the companionship of Swift. Such was the jealous care with which he preserved the letters, treasuring them as an heirloom of honour, that he would never allow them to be moved from his family seat ; and when, with his own hand, he had made careful transcript of them for me, I had to visit him at Woodbrooke to collate his copy with the originals. There I walked with him through avenues of trees which Swift was said to have planted."

As Forster's untimely death brought his Life of Swift to an abrupt close, when he had not reached by three years and more the date of the first of these letters, he made scarcely any use of the correspondence. He refers to it twice, and twice only. On his death the copy of the originals with the corrections he had made was returned to Woodbrook. It has lately come into my possession. What wonder would have seized on Swift's mind had it been foretold to him that these letters of his, after lying hidden nearly two hundred years, were first to see the light of day in an American magazine![1] America, to borrow the words of Edmund Burke, "served for little more than to amuse him with stories of savage men and uncouth manners." For him "the angel did not draw up the curtain, and unfold the rising glories of the country." He rarely mentions the settlements in his writings, and when he does it is for the most part with ignorance and contempt. He regrets that England's long and ruinous war with France had kept "Queen Anne's care of religion from reaching to her American

---

[1] Most of these letters and some few of the notes were first published in the *Atlantic Monthly*, for August, September, November, and December, 1897.

plantations. These noble countries," he continues, "stocked by numbers from hence, whereof too many are in no very great reputation for faith or morals, will be a perpetual reproach to us, until some better care be taken for cultivating Christianity among them." In his Modest Proposal for Preventing the Children of Poor People in Ireland from being a Burden to their Parents or Themselves, he says, " I have been assured by a very knowing American of my acquaintance in London, that a young healthy child, well nursed, is at a year old a most delicious, nourishing, and wholesome food, whether stewed, roasted, baked, or boiled." His strange ignorance of the natural history of America is shown in one of his papers in the *Spectator*, where he makes some Indian kings who had visited London say that "Whigs and Tories engage when they meet as naturally as the elephant and the rhinoceros."

Of Knightley Chetwode's intimacy with Swift nothing, apparently, was known to the dean's earlier biographers. Neither is this Irish squire mentioned in the more recent Life by Craik. His name is only once found in the twenty-four volumes of Nichols's edition of Swift's works. He was sprung from a family which for some centuries had its seat at Warkworth, near Banbury, where the tombs of many generations of Chetwodes can still be seen. In the reign of James I. the head of the house ruined himself in vainly asserting his claim to the barony of De Wahull. Warkworth was sold. His son went into the Church, became Dean of Gloucester, and died on the edge of the Promised Land—a bishop-elect. It was the dean's son who was Swift's correspondent. He married the daughter and heiress of Richard Brooking, of Totness, and settled in Ireland, near Portarlington, Queen's County, about fifty miles south-west of Dublin. The house which he built still stands in its main fabric. He called it Woodbrook, a name compounded of the second syllable of Chetwode and the first of Brooking. "The demesne," I am told, "is about nine hundred English acres in extent, partly woodland and partly park ; as far as one can judge, it remains much as it was laid out two hundred years ago. The timber, which is chiefly beech, is as fine as any in Ireland. Tradition connects a particular grove of beech trees near the house with the name of Swift."

Swift's first letter was written less than two months after the queen's death had broken the whole scheme of his life, and sent him back to Ireland a soured and querulous man. He who had been hand in glove with great ministers of state was now to be bullied by Dublin's archbishop and pelted by its mob. "I'll lay you a groat, Mr. Dean, I don't know you," said an Irishman to him after his fall, with whom, in the days of his prosperity, he had lived in the greatest intimacy. "I'll lay you a groat, my lord, I don't know you," Swift retorted to him, some years later, when "the whirligig of time had brought in his revenges," and he was the favourite, if not of the Crown, at all events of the people. Before those happier days came he had long "to shelter himself in unenvied obscurity." During the seven years which followed the accession of George I. Swift, to use his own words, "continued in the greatest privacy. This manner of life," he added, "was not taken up out of any sort of affection, but merely to avoid giving offence, and for fear of provoking party zeal."

> "And oh! how short are human schemes!
> Here ended all our golden dreams."

It was in these lines that he mourned the ruin which had come on himself and his friends by the death of a foolish woman. The blow surely was one which a great man should have borne without a lamentation prolonged from year to year. Of Anne no one now thinks without a certain feeling of good-natured contempt. She is the last person whom we associate with her own age. The age of Queen Anne is the age of Marlborough, of Addison and Steele, of Swift and Pope, of Prior and Gay, and not of the weak, silly woman who sat on the throne. In nothing does Swift more show that vein of baseness which ran through him than in his dejection at her death and in his estimate of her character. In his will he described her as "of ever glorious, immortal, and truly pious memory—the real nursing mother of her kingdoms." In his sixty-third year he wrote to Lord Bolingbroke, " I was forty-seven years old when I began to think of death." It was, he implies, the queen's death which first turned his thoughts towards mortality. In his lamentations over her we seem to hear "a broken worldling wail." The blow which had fallen upon him was indeed severe. His great friends had lost their places ; some of them had fled across the sea, others were in the Tower, while he himself was a suspected man. Nevertheless, why should he have been greatly troubled in mind ? Why should he have given way to "reiterated wailings"? He was the proud patriot who boasted that

> " Fair liberty was all his cry ;
> For her he stood prepared to die."

He was the Christian philosopher

> "Who kept the tenour of his mind
> To merit well of humankind."

His querulousness never came to an end, not even when he had shaken off the dread of prosecutions, and had gained a high place, not among ministers and courtiers, but in the love of the people among whom his lot was cast.

His correspondence with Chetwode covers both these periods—his downfall and his dejection, his second elevation and his haughty pride. It covers, too, the rapid growth of that terrible malady which far more even than disappointed ambition clouded his life. In the midst of all his moody discontent and his sufferings he shows that " fidelity in friendship " for which he was praised by one who knew him well. His advice and his aid were for many years at Chetwode's service. It is true that their friendship was at last dissolved in anger, but it seems likely that the chief blame of the rupture did not lie at Swift's door. In the second year of their correspondence he had to rebuke Chetwode for "an ugly suspicion"; as one "who has," he added, " more of punctilio and suspicion than I could wish." It was an ugly suspicion which parted them in the end. The squire of Woodbrook, as is shown by the last letters which passed between them, was a suspicious man. Swift, on his side, was not an easy man to deal with. "He predominated over his companions with very high ascendency, and probably would bear none over whom he could not predominate. To give him advice was, in the style of his friend Delany, 'to venture to speak to him.'"

So much by way of introduction. It is time to raise the curtain and to let Swift speak for himself.

I.

[To Knightley Chetwood Esqre. at his House near Port-Arlington in the Queen's County.]

[Pr. post.]

DUBLIN. *Sept^r* 27. 1714.

S^R [SIR],—The Person who brought me your Letter delivered it in such a Manner, that I thought I was at Court again, and that the Bearer wanted a Place ; and when I received it, I had my answer ready to give him after Pemsall, that I would do him what service I could. But I was easy when I saw your Hand at the Bottom, and then I recollected I was in Irel^d [Ireland], that the Queen was dead, the Ministry changed, and I was onely the poor Dean of St. Patricks. My Chapter joyns with me : we have consulted a Lawyer, who (as it is usuall) makes ours a very good Case ; my desires in that point are very

moderate, onely to break the Lease, and turn
out nine Singing men. I should have been with
you before this time, if it had been possible for
me to find a Horse; I have had twenty sent to
me; I have got one, but it is good for nothing;
and my English horse was so ill I was forced to
send him to Grass. There is another Evil, that
I want a stock of Hay, and I cannot get any:
I remember Prince Butler use[d] to say, By my
Soul there is not a Drop of Water in the Thames
for me. This is my Case; I have got a Fool
to lend me 50 Pounds, and now I can neither
get Hay nor Horse, and the Season of the
former is going.—However if I cannot soon get
a Horse, I will send for my own from Grass,
and in two days endeav1 to reach you; for I
hear Octobr is a very good month.

Jordan has been often telling my Agent of some
idle Pretence he has to a bitt of one of my Parishes
worth usually about 5{ll} p. ann. [five pounds per
annum], and now the Queen is dead perhaps he
may talk warmer of it. But we in possession
always answer in those Cases, that we must not
injure our Successors. Those idle claims are
usual in Irel{d}, where there has been so much
Confusion in Parishes, but they never come to
anything.

I desire my humble Service may be presented to Mrs Chetwood.

I am your most obedient

humble Servt

JON : SWIFT.

Sept. 28. This was writt last night not knowing the Post day : I now tell you that by noise and Bone-fires I suppose the Pacquets are come in with account of the King's arrivall.

NOTES ON I.

" I can serve everybody but myself," Swift wrote to Stella in the days when he was powerful at Court. " I am envied and thought in high favour, and have every day numbers of considerable men teazing me to solicit for them." Bishop Kennet describes how one morning in the ante-chamber of the palace he found him " the principal man of talk and business, and acting as a master of requests. He was promising Mr. Thorold to undertake with my Lord Treasurer that, according to his petition, he should obtain a salary of £200 *per annum*, as minister of the English Church at Rotterdam. He stopped F. Gwynne, Esq., going in with the red bag to the Queen, and told him aloud he had something to say to him from my Lord Treasurer. He turned to the fire, and took out his gold watch, and complained it was very late A gentleman said he was too fast. 'How can I help it,' says the doctor, 'if the courtiers give me a watch that won't go right?' Then he instructed a young nobleman that the best poet in England was Mr. Pope, (a Papist), who had begun a translation of Homer into English verse, for which he must have them all subscribe; 'for,' says he, 'the author *shall not* begin to print till *I have* a thousand guineas for him.' Lord Treasurer, after leaving the Queen, came through the room, beckoning Dr. Swift to follow."

Swift, in the height of his power, recorded one day in his Journal: "The Duke of Marlborough was at Court to day, and nobody hardly took notice of him." The wheel had come full circle, and Swift was as insignificant as the great Duke.

He wrote to a friend on December 24, 1736: "When, upon the Queen's death, I came to my Banishment I hardly knew two faces in the nation. . . . I cannot blame you for carrying your Son to Engl^d, which hath been chiefly your home, as it was many years mine, and might still be so had the late Queen lived two months longer."

The "singing men" of his cathedral gave him some trouble. "My amusements," he wrote to Pope, "are defending my small dominions against the archbishop and endeavouring to reduce my rebellious choir." In a letter written many years later, he said: "I am Lord Mayor of 120 houses,

I am absolute lord of the greatest cathedral in the kingdom, am at peace with the neighbouring princes, the Lord Mayor of the city and the Archbishop of Dublin ; only the latter, like the King of France, sometimes attempts encroachments on my dominions, as old Lewis did upon Lorraine."

Dr. Arbuthnot, who had lost his post of Court Physician, writing to Swift about "the terrible shock," given by the Queen's death, said : " I consider myself as a poor passenger ; and that the earth is not to be forsaken, nor the rocks removed from me. But you are certainly some first minister of a great monarch, who for some misbehaviour are condemned, in this revolution of things, to govern a chapter and a choir of singing men."

The Dean's difficulty about getting a good horse lasted many years longer. He must have mentioned it to his friends in England, for in 1718 Arbuthnot wrote to him : " There are twenty lords, I believe, would send you horses, if they knew how." In 1720 Swift wrote : " I hunted four years for horses, gave £26 for one of three years and a half old, have been eighteen months training him, and when he grew fit to ride, behold my groom gave him a strain in the shoulder, he is rowelled and gone to grass. Show me a misfortune greater in its kind." The price he paid seems high when the difference in the value of money is reckoned. Twenty years earlier, when he was a poorer man, he bought a horse for £12. In the same year, as his account-book shows, his clothes and linen cost him £18, and his washing £4. For a man who was distinguished for "the oriental scrupulosity" with which he kept himself clean, the last item seems low. In the same account "shoes and books" are entered as costing £3. These two articles seem so strangely jumbled together that I suspect "books" is a misreading of "boots."

For providing post-horses he knew of a simple expedient. More than a century later Miss Edgeworth accompanied Sir Walter Scott and his son the captain on a tour in Ireland. "When some difficulty occurred about horses Sir Walter said, 'Swift in one of his letters, when no horses were to be had, says, "If we had but a captain of horse to swear for us we should have had the horses at once;" now here we have the captain of horse, but the landlord is not moved even by him.'"

Prince Butler was Brinsley Butler. He and his brother Theophilus (afterwards first and second Barons of Newtown) were at Trinity College, Dublin, with Swift. "Brinsley" was cut down to "Prince," and "Theophilus" to "Ophy." His sayings seem to have passed current. The Duchess of Ormond, in a letter to Swift, said: "Whether there were reason or not, or as Prince Butler said, crime or no crime, the man was condemned, and a price set upon his head." Sir Walter Scott in a note describes him as "a madman who used to go about London."

THE RUINS OF LARACOR VICARAGE.

[To face page 7.

The need that Swift was under of borrowing money was caused by the heavy payments he had to make on entering on his office—£800 to his predecessor for the new residence, £150 for first-fruits, and £50 for his patent. "I shall not," he wrote, "be the better for the deanery these three years. I hope in some time they will be persuaded here [in London] to give me some money to pay off these debts." A draft of a thousand pounds upon the Exchequer, which he got through Lord Boling-broke, "was intercepted by the Queen's death. He resigned it, as he says himself, 'multa gemens,' with many a groan."

"The pretence to a bitt of one of his parishes" he thus humorously mentions in a letter to Lord Bolingbroke : "I would retire if I could ; but my country seat, where I have an acre of ground, is gone to ruin. The wall of my own apartment is fallen down, and I want mud to rebuild it, and straw to thatch it. Besides a spiteful neighbour has seized on six feet of ground, carried off my trees, and spoiled my grove." His "country seat" was his vicarage at Laracor, a small hamlet two miles from Trim. When he went to Dublin to be in-stalled as Dean of St. Patrick's he retired as soon as he could to his "one scurvy acre of ground." Thence he wrote to Vanessa : "I hate the thoughts of Dublin, and prefer a field-bed and an earthen floor before the great house there which they say is mine."

King George arrived at Greenwich on September 18th, ten days before the news reached Dublin. Lady Mary Wortley Montagu, who was at York, describes the proclamation of the King in that city : "the Archbishop walking next the Lord Mayor, and all the country gentry following, with greater crowds of people than I believed to be in York, vast acclamations, and the appearance of a general satisfaction. The Pretender afterwards dragged about the streets and burned. Ringing of bells, bonfires and illuminations, the mob crying ' Liberty and property ! ' and ' Long live King George ! ' "

Over the larger part of Ireland, not only now, but for many years later, there were only two post-days in the week. The postage, it seems, was two-pence. In 1736 Johnson's poetical friend, Dr. Madden, urging the establishment of a third post, said that "a third penny more on every letter would fully answer the additional trouble." He complained of the carelessness of the postmasters and the idleness of the post-boys. "It would do well," he continued, "to fix the hours by law, with a penalty on each postmaster of five shillings before any two Justices, and whipping for the boy, if he falls short by two hours of his time, without showing good cause."

II.

DUBLIN, *Oct^{ber} 6th* 1714.

S^R—I acknowledge both your Letters, and with any common Fortune might have spared you the Trouble of reading this by coming my self : I used to value a good Revenue, because I thought it exempted a man from the little subaltern Cares of Life ; and so it would if the Master were wise, or Servants had honesty and common Sense : A man who is new in a House or an Office has so many important Nothings to take up his time, that he can not do what he would—I have got in Hay ; but my Groom offended against the very letter of a Proverb, and stackt it in a rainy day, so that it is now smoaking like a Chimny ; my Stable is a very Hospitall for sick Horses. A Joyner who was to shelve a Room for my Library has employed a fortnight, and yet not finished what he promised in six days. One Occasion I have to triumph, that in six weeks time I have been able to get rid of a great Cat, that belonged to the late Dean, and almost poisoned the House. An old Woman under the same circumstances I can not yet get rid of, or find a Maid. Yet in Spight of all these Difficultyes, I hope to share some part of October at Wood-brook. But I scorn your Coach : for I find upon Tryall I can ride.

Indeed I am as much disquieted at the Turn of publick Affairs as you or any man can be. It concerns us Spirituall men in a tender temporall Point. Every thing is as bad as possible; and I think if the Pretender ever comes over, the present men in Power have traced traced [*sic*] him the Way— Y^r Servant is just come for this, and I am dressing fast for Prayers.

Y^r most obed^t &c.   J. S.

NOTES ON II.

"The little subaltern cares of life," that are caused by a want of money, are seen in the *Journal to Stella* to trouble Swift often. Thus, one June day, when he was lodging at Kensington, he wrote: "I was in the City till past ten at night; it rained hard, but no coach to be had. It gave over a little and I walked all the way here, and got home by twelve. I love these shabby difficulties when they are over; but I hate them because they arise from not having a thousand pounds a year." "God forbid," he wrote in his old age, "that ever such a scoundrel as Want should dare to approach me."

He thus describes his household: "You are to understand that I live in the corner of a vast unfurnished house; my family consists of a steward, a groom, a helper in the stable, a footman, and an old maid, who are all at board-wages, and when I do not dine abroad, or make an entertainment, (which last is very rare), I eat a mutton-pie, and drink half a pint of wine." The house, which had been rebuilt by his predecessor, was burnt down in 1781. It seems strange that no view was ever taken of the residence of so great a man. If there is one in existence it has escaped my inquiries.

Irish servants Swift attacked from the pulpit. "Are our goods embezzled, wasted and destroyed? is our house burnt to the ground? It is by the sloth, the drunkenness or the villainy of servants. Are we robbed and murdered in our beds? It is by confederacy with our servants. . . . Nay the very mistakes, follies, blunders and absurdities of those in our service are able to ruffle and discompose the mildest nature, and are often of such consequence as to put whole families into confusion." He traced their misconduct to "the two nurseries" from which a great number of them came. "The first is the tribe of wicked boys, wherewith most corners of this town are pestered, who haunt public doors. These, having been born of beggars, and bred to pilfer as soon as they can go or speak, as years come on, are employed in the lowest offices to get themselves bread, are practised in all manner of villainy, and when they are grown up, if they are not entertained in a gang of thieves, are forced to seek for a service. The other nursery is the bar-barous and desert part of the country, from whence such lads come up hither to seek their fortunes, who are bred up from the dunghill in idleness, ignorance, lying, and thieving."

The following advertisement, which appeared in *Pue's Occurrences* for August, 2–5, 1740, throws light on the relations between master and servant in Ireland in the days of Swift :—

"Whereas Ellen Owen, Cook Maid to Crewe Chetwood of Woodbrook in the Queen's County, Esq.; in the absence of her Master, who left her the care of his Family House, Furniture, &c., eloped from her Service the beginning of June last : This is to acquaint the publick not to Entertain or receive the said Ellen Owen into their service, she not being discharged from her Master, nor having given up the charge committed to her care. July 23, 1740.

"CREWE CHETWOOD."

Swift described his library as "a little one. A great library always makes me melancholy, where the best author is as much squeezed and as obscure as a porter at a coronation."

He was exact in his daily attendance at the cathedral service. Three weeks before the date of this letter he wrote, "I live a country life in town, see nobody, and go every day once to prayers ; and hope in a few months to grow as stupid as the present situation of affairs will require." He used to read prayers every evening to his household, but so secretly that a friend had lived with him more than six months without discovering it. " The suspicions of his irreligion," said Johnson, " proceeded in a great measure from his dread of hypocrisy ; instead of wishing to seem better, he delighted in seeming worse than he was." Lord Bolingbroke " summed up his character in this respect by saying that he was a hypocrite reversed." Nevertheless Swift had maintained that " hypocrisy is much more eligible than open infidelity and vice ; it wears the livery of religion ; it acknowledges her authority, and is cautious of giving scandal."

III.

DUBLIN *Oct*ber 20th 1714

Sr—The Bishop of Drom [Dromore] is expected this night in Town on purpose to restore his Cat, who by her perpetual noise and Stink must be certainly a whig. In complyance to yr observation of old women's tenderness to each other, I have got one as old and ugly as that the Bishop left, for the Ladys of my Acquaintance would not allow me one with a tolerable Face tho I most earnestly interceded for it. If I had considered the uncertainty of weather in our Climat, I should have made better

use of that short sunshine than I did ; but I was
amusing myself to make the Publick Hay and
neglected my own—Do you mean my Lady Jenny
Forbes that was ? I had almost forgot her. But
when Love is gone, Friendship continues. I
thought she had not at this time of day been at a
loss how to bring forth a child. I find you are
ready^{er} at kindling other peoples bonfires than y^r
own. I had one last night par maniere d'acquit, and
to save my windows.

Y^r closet of 18 foot square is a perfect Gascon-
nade. I suppose it is the largest Room in y^r House
or rather two Rooms struck out into one. I thank
you for your Present of it, but I have too many
rooms already ; I wish you had all I could spare,
tho' I were to give you money along with them.
Since you talk of your Cave de brique, I have
bought 46 dozen Bottles and want nothing but the
Circumstance of Wine to be able to entertain a
Friend. You are mistaken, I am no Coy Beauty
but rather with submission like a Wench who has
made an Assignation and when the day comes, has
not a Petticoat to appear in. I am plagued to death
with turning away and taking Servants, my Scotch
groom ran away from me ten days ago and robbed
me and several of the neighbourhood. I cannot
stir from hence till a great Vessell of Alicant is

bottled and till my Horse is in a condition to travel and my chimney piece made—I never wanted so much a little country air, being plagued with perpetual Colds and twenty Aylments yet I cannot stir at present as things stand.

I am y^r most obedient &c.

Notes on III.

The Bishop of Dromore, Dr. John Sterne, was "the late Dean" of the second letter. Swift, in earlier years, had enjoyed his "wine and conversation" in what he calls "the little room," in the Deanery. "Well, Sir," he once wrote to him, "long may you live the hospitable owner of good Bits, good Books, and good Buildings." In some lines, scratched with a diamond on a window of the Deanery House he thus describes the change caused by Sterne's promotion and his own succession :—

> "In the days of good John, if you came here to dine,
> You had choice of good meat, but no choice of good wine.
> In Jonathan's reign, if you come here to eat,
> You have choice of good wine, but no choice of good meat."

Swift was fond of wine. In his old age he wrote to a London alderman : "My chief support is French wine, which, although not equal to yours, I drink a bottle to myself every day."

"You tell us," he wrote to a friend, "your wine

is bad and that the clergy do not frequent your house, which we look upon as tautology." He laughed at Pope for his stinginess as a host. In a letter to Guy he says : "You have not forgot, 'Gentlemen, I will leave you to your wine,' which was but the remainder of a pint when four glasses were drunk. I tell that story to everybody in commendation of Mr. Pope's abstemiousness." Nevertheless he gradually fell into the same fault himself. " He was always careful of his money," writes Johnson, "and was therefore no liberal entertainer, but was less frugal of his wine than of his meat. At last his avarice grew too powerful for his kindness ; he would refuse a bottle of wine, and in Ireland no man visits where he cannot drink." Hearne, describing a feast given in 1706 by the Lord Mayor to the Duke of Marlborough, says, " The claret that was drunk cost 1s. 6d. per bottle." At the same feast the music cost £50. Mrs. Delany, writing in 1750, says that at Dundrum, "a pleasant nest of cabins by the sea-side " south-west of Downpatrick, " French white wine may be had at fivepence per bottle. We have not yet tasted it," she adds.

In his abuse of the Whigs Swift almost surpasses Johnson, who maintained that the first Whig was the devil, and that ": the Whigs of America multiply with the fecundity of their own rattlesnakes." Nevertheless, the dean said, and said with much truth, that "he was always a Whig in politics." It

was in Church matters that he was a Tory. It was
probably to an Irish Whig that he likened the cat.
"The thing we called a Whig in England," he
wrote, "is a creature altogether different from those
of the same denomination here." He adds that
Addison, when he was Secretary to the Lord-
Lieutenant, told him " that the chief managers here
were a sort of people who seemed to think that the
principles of a Whig consisted in nothing else but
damning the church, reviling the clergy, abetting
the dissenters, and speaking contemptibly of revealed
religion."

" The Ladys of my Acquaintance " were Stella
and her companion, Mrs. Dingley. " Lady Jenny
Forbes that was," the elder daughter of the second
Earl of Granard, had married Major Champagné,[1] of
Portarlington.

The bonfire that Swift kindled to save his
windows was to celebrate the coronation of George
I. In some towns in England the windows were
broken in the houses of those who joined in the
illumination. The cry of the Bristol rioters, for
instance, was, "Damn all foreign governments."
In Dublin the mob was Protestant and Hanoverian.
In Oxford next year, on Restoration Day, according to Hearne, "the people ran up and down
crying King James the Third! The true King!

[1] So the name is spelt in Burke's Peerage. Swift, *post* p. 51,
spells the name Champigné.

No usurper!" The meeting-houses of the Non-
conformists were pulled down. Thirty-nine years
later Mrs. Delany wrote : " We were ushered into
Oxford by ringing of bells, illuminations, squibs,
crackers, and bonfires, and could willingly have
spared all the bustle and roar of joy that surrounded
us. It was all for his Majesty's coronation day."

IV.

[Indorsed, "*A* pencil *note f^r Wodebrook where
he came in K. C.'s [Knightley Chetwode's] absence
dining out.*"]

Not to disturb you in the good work of a God-
father nor spoil y^r dinner, I onely design Mrs Chetwode and you would take care not to be benighted ;
but come when you will you shall be heartily
welcome to my House. The children's Tutor is
gone out and so there was no pen and ink to be
had.

WOODBROOK, *Nov^r* 6th past one in the afternoon.

V.

[Indorsed, " *This was my advice to a young
Lady.*"]

I look [*sic*] over the inclosed some time ago, and

again just now ; it contains many good Things, and wants many alterations. I have made one or two, and pointed at others, but an Author can only sett his own Things right.—Friday.

VI.

[Per messenger.]

DUBLIN. *Dec^{br}* 3. 1714

S^{R},—Mr Graves never came to me till this morning, like a vile Man as he is. I had no letters from Engl^{d} to vex me except on the publick Account ; I am now teazed by an impertinent woman, come to renew her Lease, the Baron and she are talking together—I have just squired her down, and there is at present no body with me but—yes now Mr Wall [? Walls] is come in—and now another—you must stay ;—Now I am full of company again and the Baron is in hast,—I will write to you in a Post or two. Manly is not Commiss^{nr} nor expects it. I had a very ingenious Tory Ballad sent me printed, but receiving it in a Whig house I suddenly read it, and gave it to a Gentleman with a wink, and ordered him to burn it, but he threw another Paper into the Fire. I hope to send you a Copy of it. I have seen nobody since I came. Bolton's Paten

for St. Warbraw is passed, and I believe I shall
find Difficultyes with the Chapter about a Successor
for him. I thought to give the Baron some good
Coffee, and they made it so bad, that I would
hardly give it Wharton. I here send some Snuff
to Mrs Chetwood; the Baron will tell you by what
Snatches I write this Paper. I am y^{rs} &c.

      My humble Service to Dame Plyant.

Notes on VI.

Isaac Manley was at the head of the post-office
in Ireland. Swift befriended him in the Queen's
time, though he mentions more than once that he
was accused of opening letters. Some years later
the Dean wrote: "I escaped hanging very
narrowly a month ago; for a letter from Preston,
directed to me, was opened in the post-office and
sealed again in a very slovenly manner, when
Manley found it only contained a request from a
poor curate."

Bolton was Dr. Theophilus Bolton, Chancellor
of St. Patrick's, afterwards Bishop of Clonfert and
Archbishop of Cashel. He had been appointed
Rector of St. Werburgh. Swift, in 1717, complained
of his behaviour: "He has taken every opportunity
of opposing me in the most unkind and unnecessary
manner, and I have done with him." Five years
later the Dean wrote: "Your new Bishop Bolton

was born to be my tormentor, he ever opposed me as my subject, and now has left me embroiled for want of him." In 1735, Bolton, now Archbishop, sent a kind letter to him : "If I could be put upon the old foot, as when I was your subject at St. Patrick's, I should think myself the happiest man in the world."

Swift prided himself on his skill in making coffee. To a lady who asked for a cup he said, "You shall have some in perfection ; for when I was chaplain to the Earl of Berkeley, who was in the government here, I was so poor I was obliged to keep a coffee-house, and all the nobility resorted to it to talk treason." He thereupon made the coffee himself. He gave up drinking it later in life. "My breakfast," he wrote, "is that of a sickly man, rice gruel ; and I am wholly a stranger to tea and coffee."

Of Lord Wharton, to whom he would hardly have given the bad coffee, much as he hated him, he said : "He is the most universal villain I ever knew." In the *Short Character* he drew of him, when the Earl "had some years passed his grand climacteric," he wrote : "His behaviour is in all the forms of a young man at five and twenty. Whether he walks, or whistles, or swears, or talks bawdy, or calls names, he acquits himself in each beyond a Templar of three years' standing. . . . He goes constantly to prayers in the forms of his place, and will talk bawdy and blasphemy at the chapel door. He is a Presbyterian in politics, and

an atheist in religion ; but he chooses at present to
whore with a Papist." To attacks he was indifferent. "When these papers are public," continues Swift, "it is odds but he will tell me, as he
once did upon a like occasion, 'that he is damnably
mauled'; and then, with the easiest transition in the
world, ask about the weather or time of the day."
It was Wharton's boast that by his *Lilibulero* he
had sung a king out of his three kingdoms. His
son was scarcely less profligate. "One day he
recounted to the Dean several wild frolics he had
run through. 'My Lord,' said Swift, 'let me recommend one more to you—take a frolic to be
good ; rely upon it, you will find it the pleasantest
frolic you ever were engaged in.'"

"Dame Plyant"—the name is taken from a
character in Ben Jonson's *Alchemist*—was no doubt
Chetwode's wife. It will be seen later on that she
and her husband agreed so ill that at last they
separated.

VII.

[p^r private hand.]

Jan^{ry} 3^d 17$\frac{13}{14}$

I have had a Letter of yours by me these three
weeks, which among others has lain unanswered,
because I left of my old Custom of answering Letters

before the Post day ; and it happened that upon
Post day I never had Leisure : but besides I waited
till I could hear you had gòt to Martrey.   I know
not what you observed in the publick Gazette about
that Business I was uneasy at : for I never heard
of anything, and had Letters since from the Person
chiefly concerned.   I am afraid the Dean's Field
will be quite spoiled in your Absence.   I had made
an Extract out of the Lease of Kilberry, of the
Denominations, but feared you had no Correspondents with the Baron since you left the Neighbor-
hood.   However I will here annex it.   As for the
Ballad ; I can not for my Life tell where it is at
present, but a copy shall be sent or brought to you.

I had gone thus far when Company came in, and
I was forced to leave off, and go abroad to a Christmas dinner, where I stayed till 11, and at coming
home my maid told me that one of y^r Serv^{ts} were
[*sic*] here to know whether I would go down to
Martrey, and that he will call to-morrow morning ;
therefore I resolve to finish this Let^r to night, and
am glad of the opportunity, not knowing where to
direct to you better than by Navan.   I believe you
may be out of the Peace, because, I hear almost all
our Friends are so.   I am sorry Toryes are put out
of the King's Peace : he may live to want them in
it again.   My Visitation is to be this day Sennight,

after which I soon intend for the county of Meath :
I design great Things at my Visitation, and I
believe my Chapter will joyn with me : I hear they
think me a smart Dean ; and that I am for doing
good : my notion is, that if I [*sic*] a man cannot
mend the Publick he should mend old shoes if he
can do no better ; and therefore I endeavor in the
little Sphere I am placed to do all the good it is
capable of.   As for judicious John, he is walked
off : y^r cursed good Ale ruined him.   He turned
such a Drunkard and Swaggerer, I could bear him
no longer : I reckon every visit I make you will
spoil a Servant.   I shall come with 2 Servants and
3 Horses, but a Horse and a Servt I shall leave at
Trim.   I hear an universall good Character of M^r
Davise ; but however I shall have my eye over him
and the lads.   As for news, the D——l a bitt do
I ever hear, or suffer to be told me.   I saw in a
Print that the K—— [King] has taken Care to
limit the Clergy what they shall Preach ; and that
has given me an Inclination to preach what is
forbid : for I do not conceive there is any Law yet
for it.   My humble Service to Dame Plyant.   You
talk of ye Hay but say nothing of ye Wine.   I
doubt it is not so good as at Woodbrook : and I
doubt I shall not like Martrey half so well as
Woodbrook.

Now for the Lands at Kildare.

The Mannors, Lordships and Townships of Kilberry, Castleridge and Clony—Also the Prebend of Kilberry, with the Lands, Tenements and Tythes whatsoever appertaining to the s^d Prebend, Rectory, Churches, and Towns of Kilberry, Byrt, Clony Shrowlane, Kilcoleman, Oldcourt, and Tullaghgorie, Preswelstown, Shanraghin, Tyrrellstown, Clonwonwyre, and Russelstown.

The Land without the Prebend and all those cursed Irish names is 1700 and odd acres; Supposing the Land to be a Crown an Acre at full Rent the whole is worth ...   ...   p. ann.   425   0   0

Supposing the Prebend and Tythe
                of all those hard names worth   50   0   0
                                                    _____
The whole will be worth at full rent   475   0   0
                                                    _____
                And it pays me only   120   0   0

There was a great deal of young wood which has been horribly abused.

If the Baron could contrive that I might have some account of this Land &c: he would do me a great Favor.

Notes to VII.

The Government, threatened by invasion from without and insurrection from within, had no hesita-

tion in removing Tories from the magistracy.
Three even of the English judges lost their places
on the king's accession. Two had been displaced
on the accession of Anne.

His visitation as Dean of St. Patrick's Swift thus
mentions in a letter to the Bishop of Meath : " I
have the honour to be ordinary over a considerable
number of as eminent divines as any in this kingdom
who owe me the same obedience as I owe to your
lordship, and are equally bound to attend my
visitation."

That he was "a smart Dean" is allowed by
Johnson. "To his duty as Dean he was very
attentive. He managed the revenues of his church
with exact economy. Of his choir he was eminently
careful. In his church he restored the practice of
weekly communion. He came to church every
morning."

Trim, where he was to leave a horse, is a small
town twenty miles from Dublin, pleasantly mentioned in Thackeray's lines on the Duke of
Wellington :—

> " By memory backwards borne,
>   Perhaps his thoughts did stray
> To that old house where he was born
>   Upon the first of May.

> " Perhaps he did recall
>   The ancient towers of Trim ;
> And County Meath and Dangan Hall
>   They did revisit him."

SWIFT'S WELL.

[To face page 27.

At Laracor, close by, was Swift's vicarage, where he spent some of his happiest days. In his absence it was commonly inhabited by Stella and her companion ; when he returned they moved into Trim. The garden which he laid out, the willows which he planted, the pretty walk which he made, winding along a small stream, "whose banks he smoothed," have long disappeared. Here, if he had not "a handsome house to lodge a friend," at all events he had—

> "A river at my garden's end ;
> A terrace walk, and half a rood
> Of land set out to plant a wood."

Of the vicarage nothing is standing but the fragment of an old wall. His duties as parish priest were light. " I am this minute very busy," he wrote, " being to preach to-day before an audience of at least fifteen people, most of them gentle and all simple." In a letter to the Archbishop of Dublin, he said : " It is one felicity of being among willows that one is not troubled with faction."

The limitation placed by the king on the clergy is thus described by Smollett : " Every preacher was restricted from delivering any other doctrine than what is contained in the Holy Scriptures with respect to the Trinity, and from intermeddling in any affairs of state or government." Arbuthnot, a little earlier, had written to Swift : " There is one thing in your circumstance that must make any man happy; which is a liberty to preach. For my part, I never imagine any man can be uneasy that has the opportunity of venting himself to a whole congregation once a week."

A full description of the endowments of the Dean of St. Patrick's may be found in W. M. Mason's *History of the Cathedral*, p. 26.

VIII.

DUBLIN. [private hand:] *Mar.* 31. 1715

S^r,—I have been these ten weeks resolving every week to go down to Trim, and from thence to Martry; and have not been able to compass it, tho' my Country Affairs very much required my Presence. This week I was fully determined to have been at Trim, but my Vicars hinder me, their Prosecutions being now just come to an Issue, and I cannot stir from hence till the end of April, when nothing but want of Health or Horses shall hinder me. I can tell you no news. I have read but one Newspaper since I left you. And I never suffer any to be told me. I send this by my Steward, who goes to Trim, to look after my Rents at Laracor—Pray present my most humble service to Dame Plyant; I suppose you do not very soon intend to remove to the Queen's County;

when I come to Trim I shall after a few days there, stay awhile with you, and go thence to Arthy [Athy]; and thence if possible to Connaught and half round Irel^d; I hope y^r little fire Side is well.   I am with great Truth and Esteem

Y^r most obd^t humble ser^t

J. S.

Is it impossible to get a plain easy sound trotting Horse?

NOTES ON VIII.

The vicars under whose prosecutions Swift suffered were the vicars-choral of his cathedral— the "singing-men" of his first letter.   They were twelve in number, of whom five at least were to be priests.   The Dean might punish them by mulct, suspension, or expulsion.   They were to treat him with great respect, as the following statute of the date of Charles I. shows : "Also every vicar att his goeing to read any lesson, littanies, or to the Lord's table, shall, both goeing and att his returne, expresse a civell obeydance to the Deane, or in his absence to the Sub-deane . . . and they may not presume to put on their hatts at any time in 'Nave Ecclesiæ,' or walke in the yeles [aisles] of the church in the presence of the Deane or Sub-deane with their hatts on."

Swift, in his old age, when his mind had almost

failed, wrote *An Exhortation addressed to the Sub-Dean and Chapter of St. Patrick's Cathedral.* In this he says : "Whereas it hath been reported that I gave a licence to certain vicars to assist at a club of fiddlers in Fishamble Street, I do hereby declare that I remember no such licence to have been ever signed or sealed by me ; and that if ever such pretended licence should be produced, I do hereby annul and vacate the said licence.

"Intreating my said sub-dean and chapter to punish such vicars as shall ever appear there as songsters, fiddlers, pipers, trumpeters, drummers, drum-majors, or in any sonal quality, according to the flagitious aggravations of their respective disobedience, rebellion, perfidy, and ingratitude."

Of his ignorance of public news he protests somewhat too often and too much. Some years later he wrote to Pope : "I neither know the names nor number of the Royal Family which now reigns farther than the prayer-book informs me. I cannot tell who is Chancellor, who are Secretaries, nor with what nations we are in peace or war."

IX.

DUBLIN. *April* 6th 1715

S^R,—Your Messenger brought me y^r Letter when I was under a very bad Barbers hands, meaning my own ; I sent for him up, because I heard he was something Gentlemannish, and he told me he returned to-day; so that I have onely time to thank you for y^r letter, and assure you, that bar accidents I will be in Trim in a fortnight—I detest the Price of that Horse you mention, and as for your Mare I will never trust her ; my Grandmother used to say that good Feeding never brings good Footing; I am just going to Church, and can say no more, but my humble service to Dame Plyant. I believe the fellow rather thinks me mad than is mad himself; 16^l! why tis an Estate ; I shall not be master of it in 16 years.

I thought that Passage out of Shakespear had been of my own Starting, and that the Magistrate of Martry would not have imagined it—How can you talk of going a Progress of 200 miles ?

I know nothing of any Shoes I left. I am sure they are not p^d [paid] for and so at least I shall be no loser whatever you may be. Adieu.

Notes on IX.

His young cousin, Deane Swift, an undergraduate of Oxford, made him a present of some new shaving tackle. The Dean wrote to Mrs. Whiteway : "Mr. Swift's gimcracks of cups and ball, in order to my convenient shaving with ease and despatch, together with the prescription on half a sheet of paper, was exactly followed, but some inconveniences attended: for I cut my face once or twice, was just twice as long in the performance, and left twice as much hair behind as I have done this twelvemonth. I return him therefore all his implements and my own compliments, with abundance of thanks, because he hath fixed me during life in my old humdrum way."

Whether the saying that Swift attributes to his grandmother was really hers may well be doubted. "He used to coin proverbs and pass them off for old. One day when walking in a garden he saw some fine fruit, none of which was offered him by its stingy owner. 'It was an old saying of my grandmother's,' he said, "Always pull a peach when it lies in your reach."' He accordingly plucked one, and his example was immediately followed by all the rest of the company under the sanction of that good old saying." Another day, seeing a farmer thrown from his horse into a slough, he asked him whether he was hurt. "'No,' he replied; 'but I am woundily bemired.' 'You make good the old proverb,' said Swift, 'the more dirt, the less hurt.' The man seemed much comforted with the old saying, but said he had never heard of it before; and no wonder, for the dean had made it on the occasion." In the *Journal to Stella* these sayings are often to be found. One day he complains that she writes on thin paper. "Why, that is a common caution that writing-masters give their scholars ; you must have heard it a hundred times. It is this:—

> " ' If paper be thin,
> Ink will slip in ;
> But if it be thick,
> You may write with a stick.' "

Another day he tells her and her friend that " it is an old saying and a true one—

> " ' Be you lords, or be you earls,
> You must write to naughty girls.' "

" I dined with the Secretary," he writes, " and we were to do more business after dinner ; but after dinner is after dinner—an old saying and a true, ' much drinking, little thinking.' " He quotes his grandmother when the Lord Treasurer is always asking him to dinner, but never gives him a good post in the Church. " What will this come to ? Nothing. My grandmother used to say—

> " ' More of your lining,
> And less of your dining.' "

His grandmother on the father's side came of a good stock, for she was a Dryden—first cousin of the poet's father.

According to Sir Walter Scott, " Swift never once alludes to the writings of Shakespeare. The catalogue of his library only contains the works of three dramatic authors, Ben Jonson, Wycherley, and Rowe, the two last being presentation copies from the authors." We find him, however, alluding to Shakespeare in this letter, and also in his *Journal to Stella*, where he writes: "When I expected we were all undone I designed to retire for six months, and then steal over to Laracor; and I had in my mouth a thousand times two lines of Shakespeare, where Cardinal Wolsey says—

> "'A weak old man, battered with storms of state,[1]
> Is come to lay his weary bones among you.'"

He quotes also Fluellen in a letter.

X.

To Knightley Chetwode Esq at Martry near Navan in the County of Meath.

DUBLIN. *June* 21. 1715.

I was to see Jordan, who tells me something but I have forgot it. It was, that he had a Letter ready and you were gone, or something of that kind. I had a terrible hot journey and dined with Forbes, and got here by 9. I have been much entertained with news of myself since I came here,

[1] "An old man, broken with the storms of state."

tis s^d there was another Packet directed to me, seised by the Government; but after opening several Seals it proved onely plum-cake. I was this morning with the A. Bp : [Archbishop] who told me how kind he had been in preventing my being sent to &c ; I s^d I had been a firm friend of the last Ministry, but thought it brought me to trouble my self in little Partyes without doing good, that I therefore expected the Protection of the Government and that if I had been called before them I would not have answered one Syllable or named one Person—He s^d that would have reflected on me, I answered I did not value that ; that I would sooner suffer more than let any body else suffer by me—as some people did—The Letter wch was sent was one from the great L^{dy} [Lady] you know, and inclosed in one from her Chaplin—my Friends got it, and very wisely burned it after great Deliberation, for fear of being called to swear ; for wch I wish them half hangd—I have been named in many Papers as a proclaimd for 500^{ll}. I want to be with you for a little good meat and cold Drink ; I find nothing cold here but the Reception of my Friends. I s^d a good deal more to the A. Bp : not worth telling at this distance—I told him I had several Papers, but was so wise to hide them some months ago. A Gentleman was run through in the

Play-house last night upon a squabble of their Footmen's taking Places for some Ladyes.—My most humble Service to Dame Plyant ; pray God bless her fireside.

They say the Whigs do not intend to cut of Ld. [Lord] Oxford's head but that they will certainly attaint poor Ld. Bolingbroke.

NOTES ON X.

Swift's expression "another packet" implies that two packets directed to him were seized. Mr. Craik, in his *Life of Swift*, prints a letter sent to Archbishop King, on May 15 of this year, in which the writer says : " I received yesterday a letter from Mr. Manley, giving an account of the seizing of a parcel of treasonable papers with one Jefferies directed to Dr. Swift. I acquainted my Lord-Lieutenant with it, who was very well pleased with this fresh instance of your Grace's diligence and zeal in the King's service. His excellency hopes that if there appear enough against the Doctor to justify it, he is kept in confinement, and Mr. Houghton also. I presume they are at least held to very good and sufficient bail." Smollett, in his *History*, states that when Jefferies was seized " Swift thought proper to abscond." The Archbishop, near the end of the following year, wrote to Swift, from London : " We have a strong report that my Lord Bolingbroke will return here, and be pardoned ; certainly it must not be for nothing. I hope he can tell no ill story of you." Swift repelled the insinuation that he was a Jacobite with indignation. "I am surprised to think your Grace could talk, or act, or correspond with me for some years past ; whilst you must needs believe me a most false and vile man ; declaring to you on all occasions my abhorrence of the Pretender, and yet privately engaged with a ministry to bring him in ; and therefore warning me to look to myself, and prepare my defence against a false brother, coming over to discover such secrets as would hang me."

The "great lady" was the Duchess of Ormond, whose husband had fled to France. Though Swift, to use his own words, "looked upon the coming of the Pretender as a greater evil than any we are likely to suffer under the worst Whig ministry that can be found," nevertheless by the Protestant mob of Dublin he was at this time treated as a Jacobite. He never went abroad without servants armed to protect him. In his later years he was the idol of this same rabble. "I walk the streets," he wrote, "and so do my lower friends, from whom and from whom alone, I have a thousand hats and blessings." Sheridan tells us that "he was known over the whole kingdom by the title of THE DEAN, given to him by way of pre-eminence, as it were by common consent ; and when THE DEAN was mentioned, it always carried with it the idea of the first and

greatest man in the kingdom. THE DEAN said
this; THE DEAN did that; whatever he said or did
was received as infallibly right."

Soon after the report had been spread that he
" was a proclaimed for £500," a reward of £100,000
was offered for "the Pretender dead or alive." For
the Duke of Ormond's head a reward of £10,000
was offered. The Dean had probably hidden his
papers on hearing from Erasmus Lewis, who on
November 4, 1714, wrote to him: "I send this to
acquaint you, that if you have not already hid your
papers in some private place in the hands of a trusty
friend, I fear they will fall into the hands of our
enemies."

The misconduct of footmen was common enough
in those days, in London as well as in Dublin. In
Swift's Directions to Servants "the last advice to
the footman relates to his behaviour when he is
going to be hanged."

In the *Gentleman's Magazine* for March, 1732,
complaint is made of "the numbers of footmen
every evening who are lolling over the boxes, while
they keep places for their masters, with their hats
on, play over their airs, take snuff, laugh aloud, or
hold dialogues with their brethren from one side of
the house to the other. When the audience have
resented it, they have stood on their defence, even
with menaces, till they have been turned out by
the head and shoulders." They grew bolder as
years went on, for in the same Magazine for March,

1737, is the following account of a riot raised by them in London : " The footmen, having on account of their rudeness been denied entrance into the gallery they used to have allowed them, a body of them, to the number of three hundred, armed with offensive weapons, broke open the doors of Drury Lane Theatre. They fought their way to the stage door, forced it open, and wounded twenty-five persons. Colonel De Veil being in the house attempted to read the proclamation ; but such was their violence (notwithstanding the Prince and Princess of Wales, and others of the Royal Family were there) he was obstructed in the execution of his duty. However he caused some of the ring-leaders to be seized ; and after examination sent three of them to Newgate, upon which some had the assurance to send the following letter :—

" ' *To Mr. Fleetwood, in Lincoln's Inn Fields,*
Master of Theatre, Drury Lane.

" ' Sr.

" ' We are willing to admonish you before we attempt our Design ; and Provide you will use us Civil, and Admitt us into our Gallery, which is our Property according to Formalities ; and if you think proper to Come to a Composition this way you'll hear no further ; and if not, our intention is to Combine in a Body in Cognito, And Reduce the play-house to the Ground, Valuing no Detection. we are Indemnified.'

"But a guard of fifty soldiers being appointed for several nights, the footmen made no further attempts."

When an effort was made to put an end to the custom of guests giving servants vails (presents of money), the footmen night after night raised a riot in Ranelagh Gardens, and mobbed some gentlemen who had been active in the attempt. "There was fighting with drawn swords for some hours; they broke one chariot all to pieces."

Robert Harley, Earl of Oxford, was attainted of high treason, but after an imprisonment of nearly two years in the Tower was acquitted. He had experience of the fickleness of "the many-headed multitude." "He was thought," wrote Charles Ford to Swift, "to show more joy upon proclaiming the King than was consistent with the obligation he had received from —— [probably the late Queen]. He was hissed all the way by the mob, and some of them threw halters into his coach. This was not the effect of party, for the Duke of Ormond was huzzaed throughout the whole city." On his acquittal at the end of his long imprisonment "the acclamations were as great as upon any other occasion." Bolingbroke escaped to France.

XI.

DUBLIN. *June* 28. 1715

I write to you so soon again, contrary to my
nature and Custom which never suffered me to be a
very exact Correspondent.   I find you passed y^r Time
well among Ladyes and Lyons and St. Georges
and Dragons—Yesterday's post brought us an Acc^t
that the D— of O—[Duke of Ormond] is voted to
be impeached for high Treason.   You see the Plot
thickens ; I know not the present Disposition of
People in Engl^d but I do not find myself disposed
to be sorry at this news—However in generall my
Spirits are disturbed, and I want to be out of this
Town.   A Whig of this Country now in Engl^d has
writt to his Friends, that the Leaders there talk of
sending for me to be examined upon these Impeachments ; I believe there is nothing [in] it ; but I had
this notice from one who said he saw the Letter or
saw somebody that saw it.   I write this Post to D^r
Raymd [Raymond] to provide next Sunday for M^r
Sub, so I suppose he may be at ease, and I wish I
were with him.   I hope Dame has established her
Credit with you for ever, in the point of Valor and
Hardyness—You surprise me with the Acc^t [account]
of a Disorder in y^r head ; I know what it is too well
and I think Dame does so too.   You must drink

less small beer, eat less sallad, think less, walk and drink more, I mean Wine and Ale, and for the rest, Emeticks and bitters are certainly the best Remedyes. What Legnth has the River walk to 30 foot bredth? I hope 8 thousand at least. If Sub. had no better a tast for Bief and Claret than he has for Improvemts of Land, he should provide no Dinners for me— Does Madam gamble now and then to see it? How is the Dean's field? So it cost a bottle of wine ex^{cdy} [?] to dry poor Sub. I hope he sometimes loses his eyes to please Dame. There is a Collegian found guilty of speaking some words; and I hear they design in mercy to whip or Pillory him. I went yesterday to the Courts on purpose to show I was not run away. I had warning given me to beware of a fellow that stood by while some of us were talking—It seems there is a Trade going of carrying stories to the Govrt, [Government] and many honest Folks turn the Penny by it. I can not yet leave this Place but will as soon as possible. Tom this minute brought me up word that the Baron's man was here, and that his master is in Town. I hope to see him, and give him half a breast of mutton before he goes back. He is now with a Lawyer. I believe old Lombard Street is putting out money. The Report of the Secret Committee is published. It is a large volume. I onely just saw it Manly [? at Manly's]. It is but a Part, and probably there will be as much more.

I do not believe or see one word is offered to prove their old Slander of bringing in the Pretender. The Treason lyes wholly in making the Peace. Ch. Ford is with Ld Bol—[Lord Bolingbroke] in Dauphinè within a League of Lyons, where his L^{d}ship is retired ; till he sees what the Secret Committee will do. That is now determined and his L^{d}ship [Lordship] will certainly be attainted by Act of Parl$^{m't}$ [Parliament]. The Impeachm^{ts} are not yet carryed up to the Ld^s [Lords]. I suppose they intend to make one work of it.

Notes on XI.

How correspondence between friends is too apt to come to an end Swift shows in one of the earliest of his published letters : " At first one omits writing for a little while, and then one stays a while longer to consider of excuses, and at last it grows desperate, and one does not write at all."

The Duke of Ormond was impeached on June 21st—the news reached Dublin on the 27th. In this same year Swift, writing of the attainder, says : " Now it is done, it looks like a dream to those who consider the nobleness of his birth, the great merits

of his ancestors and his own; his long unspotted
loyalty, his affability, generosity, and sweetness of
nature. I knew him long and well." That the
Dean was not "disposed to be sorry at the news"
was, I suppose, due to the belief that the attainder
of so popular a man would bring unpopularity on
the ministry. While the House of Commons without a division resolved to impeach Oxford, against
the impeachment of Ormond 187 members voted.
The Duke was safe abroad. Arbuthnot sent Swift
the news of his flight in the following passage of a
letter dated November, 1714 : " The honest gentleman at whose lodgings we wrote is gone for
France."

Dr. Raymond was the Vicar of Trim, where
Stella often was his guest. Swift in his *Journal*
wrote to her : " Dr. Raymond has sat with me two
hours, and drank a pint of ale cost me fivepence,
and smoked his pipe, and it is now past eleven that
he is just gone." A few weeks later he wrote :
" Poor Raymond just came in and took his leave of
me ; he is summoned by high order from his wife,
but pretends he has had enough of London. I
was a little melancholy to part with him. He was
so easy and manageable that I almost repent I
suffered him to see me so seldom. But he is gone,
and will save Patrick some lies in a week ; Patrick
is grown admirable at it, and will make his fortune."
Raymond was troubled with a family larger than
his means could well support. " Will Mrs. Ray-

mond never have done lying-in?" wrote Swift. "He
intends to leave beggars enough."

" Mr. Sub." was the Sub-dean of St. Patrick's.

The disorder in the head, of which Swift knew
what it was too well, marred his whole life. " I
have had my giddiness twenty-three years by fits,"
he wrote as early as 1712. Mr. Craik quotes the
report published in 1882 by Dr. Bucknill on this
disorder : " The two maladies of giddiness and
deafness from which he suffered had their common
origin in a disease in the region of the ear, to
which the name of *Labyrinthine vertigo* has been
given." He was, however, well advanced in life
before these disorders attacked him at the same
time. In 1734 he said : " It is only of late years
that they have begun to come together." " I got
my giddiness," he said, " by eating a hundred
golden pippins at a time." On this Johnson re-
marks, " The original of diseases is commonly
obscure. Almost every boy eats as much fruit as
he can get without any great inconvenience."
Thinking little, exercise, and wine were Swift's
chief remedies. *Vive la bagatelle* was his favourite
maxim. He was like Johnson in thinking weather
and seasons of slight importance. " I never impute
any illness or health I have to good or ill weather,
but to want of exercise, or ill air, or something I
have eaten, or hard study, or sitting up ; and so I
fence against those as well as I can : but who a
deuce can help the weather ? "

Another time he wrote: " Fig for your physician and his advice, Madam Dingley: if I grow worse, I will; otherwise I will trust to temperance and exercise; your fall of the leaf : what care I when the leaves fall? I am sorry to see them fall with all my heart; but why should I take physic because leaves fall off from trees? that won't hinder them from falling. If a man falls from a horse, must I take physic for that? Use exercise and walk, spend pattens and spare potions, wear out clogs and waste claret." He did not recommend wine to all people. Most of his male friends took too much. Pulteney wrote to him : " I will follow your rules of rising early, eating little, dancing less, and riding daily."

On July 7 of this year the Archbishop of Dublin wrote to Addison : "'Tis plain there's a nest of Jacobites in the college; one was convicted last term ; two are runaways, and, I believe, bills are found against one or two more." A master of arts was expelled for making a copy of the pamphlet *Nero Secundus*, and two bachelors of arts and two students for speaking disrespectfully of the King. Of the whipping or pillory with which Swift's "collegian " was threatened I can find no mention. Five years earlier three students " had offered great indignities to the statue of William III. Two of them were expelled from the University, and were condemned to six months' imprisonment, to pay a fine of £100 each, and to be carried to College-green, and there to stand before the statue for half an hour with this inscription on his breast: 'I stand here for defacing the statue of our glorious deliverer, the late King William.'" The fine was reduced to five shillings, and the public exposure was remitted when it was shown that "they had already suffered about three months' imprisonment, in miserable circumstances, to the great hazard of their health." The prison was a noisome den, and the gaoler a cruel tyrant. Those committed for trial, unless they paid a daily fee to the keeper, were often stripped of their clothes by the common hangman and turned into the felons' room, the stench of which was insupportable. Many died of want, being left without food for several days. The keeper's salary was £10 a year; but a Parliamentary document shows that in the year 1729, partly by extortion, and partly by the sale of strong drink to the prisoners, he made £1,153 in addition. He was dismissed from office. This miserable den lasted till 1773, when it was rebuilt. The new prison had one drawback, as we are told in a book published soon after its erection: "The chapel, from its situation in the upper floor, is very difficult of access to the prisoners who are in irons." The severity shown to the students did not scare away the followers of the Pretender. On July 6, 1727, the Primate Boulter wrote: "The power the Provost has is indeed beyond anything any Head of a College has in Oxford; but is all little enough to keep the College here from being a seminary of Jacobitism."

Mrs. Delany, writing in 1751, of "the Lord-Lieutenant's parading on King William's birthday, whose memory is idolised here almost to superstition," continues : "The Duke's equipage and the nobility that attended him were very fine, and all the horses decked out with orange-coloured ribbons : there is a statue of King William before the Parliament House, and they tour round it and round Stephen's Green."

The Secret Committee of the House of Commons had examined into the negotiations for the Treaty of Utrecht. As the result, Oxford, Bolingbroke, and Ormond were impeached. "You know," Swift wrote to Pope, "how well I loved both Lord Oxford and Bolingbroke, and how dear the Duke of Ormond is to me. Do you imagine I can be easy while their enemies are endeavouring to take off their heads? 'I nunc, et versus tecum meditare canoros.'"

When the Tories were still in power, Swift wrote to Archbishop King, from London : "I do not think any one person in the Court or ministry here designs any more to bring in the Pretender than the Great Turk." Into the plots of Atterbury, Bolingbroke, and Ormond he was never admitted.

Charles Ford was of Wood Park, near Dublin. On July 1, 1712, Swift wrote in his *Journal to Stella:* "I have made Ford Gazetteer, and got

£200 a year settled on the employment by the Secretary of State, besides the perquisites. It is the prettiest employment in England of its bigness; yet the puppy does not seem satisfied with it. I think people keep some follies to themselves, till they have occasion to produce them. He thinks it not genteel enough, and makes twenty difficulties. 'Tis impossible to make any man easy." Gay, in *Mr. Pope's Welcome from Greece*, calls him "joyous Ford." Swift wrote verses on his birthday. Bolingbroke, in his *Letter to Sir William Windham*, says: "I retired into Dauphiné to remove the objection of residence near the Court of France." He goes on to mention a person sent to him from the Jacobite party who arrived in the beginning of July, 1715. It seems likely that this person was Ford.

The impeachments were carried up to the House of Lords, on July 9 against Oxford, on August 6 against Bolingbroke, and on August 8 against Ormond. Addison, who owed much to the Duke, announced his intention to be absent from the House "as by accident, if this impeachment goes on."

XII.

Dublin *July* 7. 1715.

I had y^r Letter t'other day by Mr Foxcroft who was so kind to call on me this morning, but would

not stay and dine with me tho' I offered him Mutton
and a Bottle of Wine.—I might have been cheated
of my Gingerbread for any thing you s^d [said] in
your letter, for I find you scorn to take notice of
Dame's kind Present; but I am humbler and signify
to her that if she does not receive by M^r. Foxcroft
a large tin pot well crammd with the D. of Omds.
snuff, holding almost an ounce, she is wronged.
I wish Loughlin had not been mistaken when he
saw me coming into your Court—I had much rather
come into it than. into the Court of Engl^d—I used
formerly to write Letters by bits and starts as you
did when Loghlin thought I was coming; and so
now I have been interrupted these 3 hours by company, and have now just eaten a piece of Bief Stake
spoiled in the dressing, and drunk a Cup of Sour
Ale, and return to finish my Letter; Walls sate by
me while I was at my dinner, and saw me finish it
in five minutes, and has left me to go home to a
much better. . . . Sure you stretch ye Walk when
you talk of 5000 foot, but y^r Ambition is to have
it longer than M^r. Rochfort's Canal, and with a little
expense it will be made a more beautifull thing.
Are you certain that it was Madam's green Legs
you saw by the River Side, because I have seen in
England a large kind of green Grass hopers, not
quite so tall but altogether as slender, that frequent

low marishy grounds. The Baron told me he was employed here, by you in an Affair of Usury (of wch. I give you Joy) but did not tell me the particulars. I believe the Affair of y^r English Uncle is true, I have had it from many Hands. How is that worse than the B^p. [Bishop] of London's Let^r. [Letter] to his Clergy and their Answer, both owning that the Tumults were in order to bring in Popery and Arbitrary Power—a Reproach which the Rabble did not deserve ; and has done us infinite hurt. I have not seen the Articles ; I read no news and hear little. There is no mercy for the poor Collegian : and indeed as he is s^d. to have behaved himself, there could none be expected. The Report is printed here but I have not read it. I think of going for Eng^d. (if I can get leave) when L^d. Sund [Lord Sunderland] comes over, but not before unless I am sent for with a Vengeance. I am not much grieved at y^r. being out of the Peace ; I heard something of it the day I left you, but nothing certain. Major Champigné has hard usage, and I am truly concerned for him and his Lady. I am told here that some of our Army is to be transported for Eng^d. I had a Letter this Day from thence, from the Person who sent me one from a Lady, with great Satisfaction that hers to me was not seized. That Letter talks doubtfully of the D.

Ormd. that the Parlmt. resolves to carry matters to the highest Extreems, and are preparing to impeach the D. Shrows^{b.} which the K. [King] would not suffer at first, but at length has complyed with. That Prior is kept closer than Greg, to force him to accuse Ld. Oxfrd tho' he declares he knows nothing ; and that it is thought he will be hanged if he will not be an Evidence, and that Ld. Oxf^{d.} confounds them with his Intrepidity &c.

I think neither of y^{r.} Places is remote enough for me to be att, and I have some Project of going further, and am looking out for a Horse ; I believe you will be going for Engl^{d.} by the Time I shall be ready to leave this ; hasty foolish Affairs of the Deanery keep me thus long here. My humble Service to Dame, pray God bless her and her Fireside. The Baron gave me hopes of doing something about Kilberry. Did he tell you how I pulled Toms Locks the wrong way for holding a Plate under his Armpitt and what cursed Bacon we had with our Beans? Adieu.

NOTES ON XII.

Swift often mentions snuff in his *Journal to Stella.* "April 9, 1711. My head is pretty tolerable, but every day I feel some little disorders ; I have left off snuff since Sunday, finding myself much worse after taking a great deal at the Secretary's." "April 14. My head is still wrong, but I have had no formal fit, only I totter a little. I have left off snuff altogether. I have a noble roll of tobacco for grating, very good." "June 7. Are you as vicious in snuff as ever? I believe, as you say, it does neither hurt nor good; but I have left it off, and when anybody offers me their box I take about a tenth part of what I used to do, and then just smell to it, and privately fling the rest away: I keep to my tobacco still, as you say, but even much less of that than formerly, only mornings and evenings, and very seldom in the day." He never smoked, but "he used to snuff up cut and dry tobacco, which sometimes was just coloured with Spanish snuff. He would not own that he took snuff."

Archdeacon Walls' vicarage has been made famous in Swift's verses, *On the Little House by the Churchyard of Castlenock.* It was so small that no one guessed it was for human habitation.

"The vicar once a week creeps in,
  Sits with his knees up to his chin;
  Here cons his notes and takes a whet,
  Till the small ragged flock is met.

  The doctor's family came by,
  And little miss began to cry;
  Give me that house in my own hand!
  Then madam bade the chariot stand,
  Call'd to the clerk, in manners mild,
  Pray reach that thing here to the child:

That thing, I mean, among the kale ;
And here's to buy a pot of ale.
The clerk said to her in a heat,
What ! sell my master's country seat,
Where he comes every week from town ;
He would not sell it for a crown."

Swift recorded in his *Journal to Stella* that the
Archdeacon had come to London on a five days'
visit.   " He says he and his wife will come here for
some months next year ; and, in short, he dares not
stay now for fear of her.   He told me he was just
getting on horseback for Chester.   He has as much
curiosity as a cow."

By " canal," in Swift's day, and long afterwards,
was almost always meant—to use Johnson's defi-
nition—"a basin of water in a garden."   " Canals,"
as we now use the term, were called " navigations,"
whence comes " navvy."

The spelling " marishy " for " marshy " was common enough.   Thus, in Swift's *Rhapsody*, where he
shows how—

> " epithets you link
> In gaping lines to fill a chink,"

he says they are—

> " Like a bridge that joins a marish
> To moorlands of a different parish."

In *The Windsor Prophecy*—a poem which probably far more than *The Tale of a Tub* lost Swift his

bishoprick—he described the Bishop of London (at that time Bishop of Bristol) as having "a saint at his chin and seal at his fob." The "saint," I suppose, was the bands he wore as a priest ; the seal he wore as Lord Privy Seal. He was one of the last Churchmen in England—perhaps the very last—who held high political office. Swift rejoiced in his appointment. "The Whigs," he wrote, "will fret to death to see a civil employment given to a clergyman. It was a very handsome thing in my Lord-Treasurer, and will bind the Church to him for ever."

The Bishop in his Letter to his Clergy had not gone quite so far as Swift says. "The disturbances," he had written, "will prove in the end introductive of Popery and Arbitrary Power."

"Rabble," and "behaved himself," which are found near together in this letter, may be illustrated by the following note by John Nichols and Sir Walter Scott : "Dr. Swift could not endure to hear the phrase *behaved*—*behaved what ?* he would say with some emotion. He once gave Deane Swift an account of his rebuking Lord Bathurst for this, and that my Lord promised him not to be guilty of the like for the future. To this (writes Scott) I have to add that Mrs. Pendarves mentioned to a lady that one of the greatest bursts of Swift's displeasure she ever incurred was by the use of the word *mob*. 'Never let me hear you use that word again,' said the Dean with great anger.

'What, then, should I say?' '*Rabble*, to be sure,' was Swift's reply."

Lord Sunderland was Lord-Lieutenant. He never went over to Ireland. "It may be thought a blemish in his character," wrote Swift, "that he has much fallen from the height of those republican principles with which he began; for in his father's lifetime, while he was a member of the House of Commons, he would often, among his familiar friends, refuse the title of Lord (as he has done to myself) swear he would never be called otherwise than Charles Spencer, and hoped to see the day when there should not be a peer in England. His understanding at the best is of the middling size; neither has he much improved it, either in reality, or, which is very unfortunate, even in the opinion of the world, by an overgrown library." Evelyn described him as "a very fine scholar," and his library as "incomparable." His son Charles, who succeeded to the Dukedom of Marlborough, took the "overgrown library" to Blenheim, where it remained for a century and a half. In five sales held between December 1881, and March 1883, it was scattered to the four quarters of heaven.

Major Champigné's father-in-law, the Earl of Granard, was one of the few Irish Protestant peers who had sided with James II. He had been imprisoned in the Tower of London by William III. The son-in-law, no doubt, was suspected of being a Jacobite.

" The D. Shrows_b." was the Duke of Shrewsbury.   Swift's spelling indicates the proper pro-
nunciation of the name of the town.   " I hope you
say Shrewsbury," an old gentleman once said to
me, pronouncing the first syllable so that it would
rhyme with *blows*, and not with *news*.   The Duke,
though he was accused in the Report of the Secret
Committee, was not impeached.   He once wrote to
Lord Somers : " Had I a son, I would sooner breed
him a cobbler than a courtier, and a hangman than
a statesman."

The Earl of Oxford, in the third article of his
impeachment, is described as having " sent Matthew
Prior, an instrument and creature of his own, into
France for the carrying on his separate and dangerous
negotiations."   Prior had been one of the Commis-
sioners by whom the Peace of Utrecht was signed.
Addison, writing on June 16, mentioning the close
confinement which the poet suffered, said it was
inflicted " in hopes to fetch the truth out of him ;
for I hear he has hitherto been very dry in his
evidence."   Prior, in his humorous *Down Hall*,
written this same year, describing a long ride he
and a friend took into Essex, says :—

> " But what did they talk of from morning till noon ?
>   Why, of spots in the sun, and the man in the moon ;
>   Of the Czar's gentle temper, the stocks in the city,
>   The wise men of Greece and the Secret Committee."

Many a day was to pass before he had another

ride, for he was kept in custody more than two years.

William Gregg, who in 1708 was a clerk in the office of the Secretary of State, being detected in treasonable correspondence with France, was condemned to death. While lying under sentence he was examined in Newgate by "seven lords of the Whig party." It was always said that had he implicated the Secretary (Harley, afterwards Earl of Oxford) his life would have been spared. He was respited from time to time, but he persisted in taking the whole guilt upon himself. At the end of a hundred days he was hanged.

Shortly after the date of this letter, Swift wrote to the Earl of Oxford, then a prisoner in the Tower, "making you," he says, "the humblest offers of my poor service and attendance. It is the first time I ever solicited you in my own behalf; and if I am refused, it will be the first request you ever refused me."

When he tells Chetwode, "I think neither of your places is remote enough for me to be att," it looks as if, to use Smollett's word, he meant to "abscond."

Dr. Johnson was more patient with his black servant, Frank, than the Dean was with his Irish Tom. Miss Reynolds tells us how "one day, as his man was waiting at Sir Joshua's table, the Doctor observed with some emotion that he had the salver under his arm." The emotion did not express itself in hostile acts.

XIII.

Aug. 2ᵈ 1715.

Considering how exact a Correspondent you are, and how bad a one I am my self, I had clearly forgot whether you had answered my last Letter, and therefore intended to have writt to you today whether I had heard from you or no: because Mᵣ Warburton told me you were upon yᵣ return to Martry. Tho it be unworthy of a Philosopher to admire at any thing, and directly forbidden by Horace, yet I am every day admiring at a thousand things. I am struck at the D. of O—— flight. A great Person here in Power read us some Letters last night importing that he was gone to the Pretender, and that upon his first Arrivall at Calais he talked of the K. only as Elector &c. But this is laughed at, and is indeed wholly unlike him, and I find his Friends here are utterly ignorant where he is, and some think him still in Englᵈ—*Aug.* 4. I was interrupted last post; but I just made a Shift to write a few words to the Baron. The Story of an Invasion is all blown off; and the Whigs seem to think there will be no such Thing. They assure us of the greatest Unanimity in Englᵈ to serve the K. and yet they continue to call the Toryes all Jacobites. They say they cannot imagine why any Tory should be angry, since there never was the

least Occasion given : and particularly they cry up
their Mercy shown to Bingley.   There is no news
of any more People gone off : tho' Ld. Shrews.ᵇ was
named.   The Suspending the Habeas Corpus Act
has frightened our Friends in Engl.ᵈ   I am heartily
concerned for poor Jo, and should be more so if he
were not swallowed up by his Betters.

Give my Service to Dame Plyant, and desire her
to let you know what quantity of Cherryes she has
for Brandy ; you may steep them in just enough to
keep them alive, and I will send you some very
good if I can and you will tell me how much.   But
here I want Jo.   I hope Dame found the boys well
and that she gave them good Counsell upon the
Subject of Gooseberryes and Codlings for I hear
the eldest had been a little out of order.

I am glad to hear you and the Doc.ᵗʳ [Doctor] are
grown so well together, and was not M.ʳˢ R. the
civilest thing in the world ?   I find you intend to
take some very sudden Resolution, and truly I was
like to be as sudden for I was upon the Ballance
two hours whether I should not take out a License
of Absence immediately upon a Letter I received ;
but at last I thought I was too late by a week for
the Design ; and so I am dropt again into my old
Insipidness : And the weather has been so bad, that
together with my want of a Horse, and my Steward

using one Every day about my Tythes, I have not
been a Mile out of Town these 5 weeks, except
once on foot.

I hear Major Champigny was left half pay; and
consequently that he will now have whole : so that
he may yet eat bread.

God preserve you and Dame and the fire-side,
believe me ever

entirely y^{rs} &c.

Notes on XIII.

Warburton was the curate at Laracor, "a gentleman of very good learning and sense who has
behaved himself altogether unblamably," as Swift
described him to the Archbishop.

> "Nil admirari prope res est una, Numici,
>   Solaque quæ possit facere et servare beatum."
>
> Horace, *Epistles* i. 6, 1.
>
> "Not to admire is all the art I know,
>   To make men happy and to keep them so."
>
> Pope, *Imitations.*

Swift could not long have doubted that Ormond
spoke of King George as Elector of Hanover, for
on landing in France the Duke joined the Pretender's party. He had in vain urged Lord Oxford to
fly with him. "Farewell, Oxford, without a head,"
he said. Oxford answered, "Farewell, duke,
without a duchy. The duke lost his duchy, but

Oxford kept his head and his earldom.   Hearne, on August 17 of this year, saw at Oxford "an officer beating up for Volunteer dragoons.   When he came against Balliol College, and was making his proclamation, a vast crowd of people surrounded him, amongst which were many scholars of Balliol College, and some too of other colleges, who hissed him, and cried out 'an Ormond, an Ormond. Down with the Round-heads, down with the Round-heads.   Down with them, down with them, down with them, down to the ground.'"   In 1743 Lady Mary Wortley Montagu found the Duke at Avignon.   "He lives here," she writes, "in great magnificence, is quite inoffensive, seems to have forgotten every part of his past life, and to be of no party."

Two days before Swift wrote "the Story of an Invasion is all blown off," the Earl of Mar had stolen away from London to raise the Highlands for King James.

It was Walpole's policy to identify Tories with Jacobites.   Bolingbroke complained that the ministry "frequently throw out that every man is a friend to the Pretender who is not a friend to Walpole."

Lord Bingley, who in 1713 had been appointed ambassador-extraordinary to Spain, and is named in the Report of the Secret Committee, was not impeached.   Ford wrote to Swift a day or two after the proclamation of the King: "Last night my Lord Bingley was beaten by mistake, coming out of his house. I doubt he has disobliged both sides so much that neither will ever own him ; and his enemies tell stories of him that I shall not believe till I find you allow them."

"Poor Jo" was Joseph Beaumont, "an eminent tallow-chandler in Trim." He is

" The grey old fellow, poet Joe,"

in Swift's verses on Archdeacon Walls' house. " I received," wrote Swift to Stella, "three pair of fine thread stockings from Jo lately. Pray thank him when you see him ; and that I say they are very fine and good. I never looked at them yet, but that's no matter." He was a " projector," who hoped to win the government reward for the discovery of a method of ascertaining the longitude. His disappointment, it was believed, turned his brain, and he made away with himself. Swift said that he had known only two projectors, one of whom ruined himself, and the other hanged himself.

Jeremy Bentham looked with indignation on Swift's frequent attacks on projectors. " I have sometimes been tempted," he wrote, " to think that were it in the power of laws to put *words* under proscription, as it has put men, the cause of inventive industry might perhaps derive scarcely less assistance from a bill of attainder against the word *project* or *projectors* than it has derived from the act authorising the grant of patents. I should add, however, ' for a time,' for even then the envy and

vanity and wounded pride of the uningenious herd
would sooner or later infuse their venom into some
other word, and set it up as a new tyranny to hover,
like its predecessor, over the birth of infant genius,
and crush it in its cradle."

Swift, I believe, had thought of taking out a
Licence of Absence from his Deanery, that he
might visit the Earl of Oxford in the Tower. As
I have shown, he had on July 19th offered him his
" poor service and attendance." In his letter to
Chetwode of the following December 17th (*post*
p. 70) he refers to this intention. He was a
faithful friend. A year earlier, when the Earl
was falling from power, he wrote to him : " If I
only look toward myself, I could wish you a private
man to-morrow . . . and then you would see whether
I should not with much more willingness attend you
in a retirement, whenever you please to give me
leave, than ever I did at London or Windsor."

The Dean began his correspondence with his
friend with such briskness that his first thirteen
letters were written within a period of little more
than ten months. We are now coming to a great
gap ; for in the next three years he wrote but twice,
—once to Mrs. Chetwode after her husband had left
for England, and once to Chetwode himself at an
address in London. Between December 17, 1715,
and September 2, 1718, at which latter date we
find Chetwode once more in London, we have not

a single letter. In the interval he had been out of the country. I am informed by the present owner of Woodbrooke that " he was a great Jacobite, and found it well to spend a good deal of his time abroad. In the library here, there are many books bought by him in different foreign towns." If on his travels he heard from Swift, it is likely enough that on his way home he destroyed the letters, for fear of bringing his friend into trouble. So strict was the search after Jacobite papers that the coffin of Bishop Atterbury, who died in France, was opened in England, whither his body was brought for burial, in the expectation that in it would be found treasonable correspondence.

XIV.

[*To Mrs. Chetwode.*]

Oct. 7. 1715.

MADAM,—I find you are resolved to feed me wherever I am. I am extremely obliged to your Care and Kindness, but know not how to return it other wise than by my Love and Esteem for you. I had one Letter from Mr Chetwode from Chester, but it came late, and he talked of staying there onely a Week. If I knew where to write to him I would. I said a good deal to him before he went. And I

believe he will keep out of harms way in these
troublesome Times. God knows what will become
of us all. I intend when the Parl^mt [Parliament]
meets here, to retire some where into the Country:
Pray God bless and protect you, and your little fire
side: believe me to be Ever with true Esteem
Madam

Your most obed^t humble Servt

J. SWIFT.

NOTES ON XIV.

Chester, or rather Park Gate, a few miles farther
down the Dee, was the usual port of embarkation
for Ireland. It was from Chester that Milton's
Lycidas sailed, and it was at Chester that the poet
Parnell died on his way home. Swift arriving
there from London on June 6, 1713, wrote to
Stella: "I am come here after six days. A noble
rider, faith! and all the ships and people went off
yesterday with a rare wind. This was told me to
my comfort upon my arrival. Having not used
riding these three years made me terrible weary;
yet I resolve on Monday to set out for Holyhead, as
weary as I am. I will be three days going to Holyhead; I cannot ride faster say what you will. I am
upon Stay-behind's mare. I have the whole inn to
myself. I would fain scape this Holyhead journey;
but I have no prospect of ships."

He wrote at least three epigrams on the windows of his inn at Chester, the best of which is the following :—

> "The church and clergy here, no doubt,
> Are very near akin ;
> Both weather-beaten are without,
> And empty both within."

Mrs. Pendarves, better known as Mrs. Delany, in 1731, wrote from Chester, where she was waiting for a fair wind for Dublin: "At dinner-time our company meet, and we pay a shilling a-head for our meal, and find our own wine ; we are very well provided for. We have secured places in the *Pretty Betty.* The best cabin Mrs. Donnellan and I have taken to ourselves, and are to pay five guineas." In 1747 she wrote : " Park Gate consists of about fifty or sixty houses in an irregular line by the water side ; the River Dee runs from Chester, but is not navigable further than to this place."

According to her " the passage was seldom more than forty hours, and often not much more than half that time." In 1754 she crossed in thirteen hours, "a surprisingly quick passage, but a very rough. All on board excessively sick."

How troublesome these times were Swift shows in a letter written a little later. The parliament sitting in Dublin had passed a bill authorising the government " to imprison whom they please for three months, without any trial or examination. I expect," continues Swift, "to be among the first of those upon whom this law will be executed. I am gathering up a thousand pounds, and intend to finish my life upon the interest of it in Wales." Of the Irish parliament he always spoke with scorn. He described the members as "those wretches here who call themselves a parliament. They imitate the English parliament after the same manner as a monkey does a human creature." When it met in 1735, he wrote, "I determine to leave the town as soon as possible, for I am not able to live within the air of such rascals." "The last work of thought or labour which he attempted" was *The Legion Club*—a poem in which he attacked the parliament in such verses as the following :—

> " As I stroll the city, oft I
> See a building large and lofty,
> Not a bow-shot from the College ;
> Half the globe from sense and knowledge.
>
> .   .   .   .
>
> Tell us what the pile contains,
> Many a head that holds no brains.
> These demoniacs let me dub
> With the name of Legion Club.
> Such assemblies, you might swear,
> Meet when butchers bait a bear ;
> Such a noise and such haranguing,
> When a brother thief is hanging.
> Such a rout and such a rabble
> Run to hear Jack-pudding gabble."

Lady M. W. Montagu, writing of Irish titles of nobility, says : " Ever since I knew the world Irish patents have been hung out to sale like the laced and embroidered coats in Monmouth Street, and bought up by the same sort of people ; I mean those who had rather wear shabby finery than no finery at all."

It is said that Henry Flood " first taught Ireland that it had a Parliament." He became a member in 1759.

XV.

[*To Knightley Chetwode Esqr. at ye Pell-mel Coffee house in Pell-mel—London.*]

Decr. 17. 1715.

I have had 3 Lett^{rs} [Letters] from you, one from Chester, another round a Printed Paper, and the 3rd of the 6th instant : The first I could not answer for it came late, and you s^{d} [said] you were to leave Chester in a week, neither did I know how to direct to you till y^{r} 2nd came, and that was so soon followed by the 3rd that now I answer both together. I have been miserably ill of a cruell cold, beyond the common pains and so as to threaten me with ill consequences upon my health : else you should have heard from me 3 weeks sooner. I have been 10 days and am still at Mr Grattan's 4 miles from the Town, to recover myself ; and am now in a fair way—I like the Verses well. Some of them are

very well tho' ag^st [against] my Friends : but I am
positive The Town is out in their Guess of the
Author.   I wonder how you came to see the Dr—n
[Dragon] for I am told none of his nearest Relations have that Liberty, nor any but his sollicitors.
Had I been directed to go over some months ago, I
might have done it, because I would gladly have
been serviceable but now I cannot : and agree with
you and my other Friends that I am safer here.   I
am curious to know how he carryes himself, whether
he is still easy and intrepid : whether he thinks he
shall lose his Head, or whether it is generally thought
so—I find you have ferreted me out in my little
private Acquaintance, but that must be entre nous.
The best of it is you cannot trace them all.   My
service to them, and say I [would] give a great deal
to be among you.   I do not understand the Rebus.
I would apply it to myself, but then what means
narrow in flight?   I am sorry at heart for poor
Ben : He had in his Life been so Splenetick that it
was past a Jest : He should ride, and live in the
Country and leave of his Trade, for he is rich
enough.   As much as I hate News, I hear it in
spight of me, not being able to govern the Tongues
of y^r Favorite and some others ; we are here in
horrible Fears, and make the Rebells ten times
more powerfull and the Discontents greater than I

hope they really are. Nay 'tis said the Pretender is landed or landing with L^d [Lord] knows how many thousands. I always knew my Friend Mr Attorney would be as great as he could in all changes. When Cole of the Oaks comes to Town assure him of my humble Service and that when Storms are over I will pass some time with his Leave among his Plantations. Dame Plyant and I have had some Commerce, but I have not been able to go there, by foolish Impediments of Business here. She has been in pain about not hearing from you. I lately heard your Boys were well. The Baron called to see me here in the Country yesterday, and s^d you had lately writt to him. There is one period in y^r Letter very full of kind Expressions, all to introduce an ugly Suspicion of Somebody that told you I know not what. I had no Acquaintance with you at all till I came last to this Kingdom : and tis odd if I should then give my self the Liberty of speaking to y^r Disadvantage. Since that time you have used me so well, that it would be more than odd if I gave myself that Liberty. But I tell you one thing, that when you are mentioned by my self or any body else, I presently add some Expressions, that he must be a rude Beast indeed who would lessen you before me, so far am I from doing it myself, and I should avoid it more to you than another, because you are a man anxious to be informed, and have more of Punctilio [?] and Suspicion than I could wish. I would say thus much to few men. Because generally I expect to be trusted, and scorn to defend my self: and the Dr—n thought it the best Compliment to him he ever heard, when I said I did not value what I sᵈ to him, nor what I sᵈ of him. So much upon this scurvy Subject. You may direct to S. H. at Mʳˢ Holt's over agˢᵗ the Church in Brides Street. The Parlᵐᵗ here are as mad as you could desire them; all of different Partyes are used like Jacobites and Dogs. All Conversation with different Principles is dangerous and Troublesome. Honest People get into Corners, and are as merry as they can. We are as loyall as our Enemyes, but they will not allow us to be so—If what they sᵈ were true, they would be quickly undone: Pray keep yʳself out of harms way: 'Tis the best part a private man can take unless his Fortune be desperate or unless he has at least a fair Hazzard for mending the Publick. My humble Service to a much prouder man than my self; I mean yʳ Uncle. Dʳ Pr—— showed me a letter from you about 3 weeks ago: He is well I suppose for I am a private country Gentleman, and design to be so some days longer. Believe me to be ever with great Truth and Esteem yʳˢ etc.

I direct to the Pell mell Coffee house, because you mention changing Lodgings.

Notes on XV.

"I am to meet our club at the Pall Mall coffee-house," wrote Arbuthnot to Swift, "where we cannot fail to remember you."

Mrs. Delany, in 1746, having received in Dublin a letter posted in Gloucester seven days earlier, speaks of its having made "a swift passage." In 1752 she mentions that two letters posted at different times were both twenty days coming.

The Grattans are mentioned by Swift in the following passage in a letter to Lady Betty Germain, dated June 15, 1736. The Duke of whom he speaks was the Duke of Dorset, Lord-Lieutenant of Ireland : "I writ to, and told my Lord Duke, that there was a certain family here called the Grattans, and that they could command ten thousand men ; two of them are parsons, as you Whigs call them ; another is Lord Mayor of this city."

"The Dean," writes Sir Walter Scott, "was fond of pranks which bordered on childish sports. It will hardly be believed that he sometimes used to chase the Grattans, and other accommodating friends, through the large apartments of the Deanery, and up and down stairs, driving them like horses, with his whip in his hand, till he had accomplished his usual quantity of exercise." Dr. Delany gives a pleasant account of the Grattans. "They had a little house, and their cousin Jackson another, near the city; where they cultivated good humour, and cheerfulness, with their trees and fruits and sallets (for they were all well skilled in gardening and planting) and kept hospitality, after the example of their fathers." The statesman, Henry Grattan, was the grandson of one of the brothers. Sir James Mackintosh, who met him at Holland House, wrote of him in his Journal: "There is nothing so odd, so gentle, and so admirable; his sayings are not to be separated from his manner."

"The Dragon," wrote Swift, "was Lord Treasurer Oxford, so called by the Dean by contraries; for he was the mildest, wisest and best minister that ever served a prince." He was at this time a prisoner in the Tower. "He is without shadow of change," wrote Arbuthnot; "the greatest example of an unshaken tranquillity of mind that ever I yet saw, seeming perfectly well satisfied with his own conduct in every particular. You know we have often said that there is but one dragon *in rerum natura*. I do not know what he thinks, but I am perfectly well satisfied that there will not be that one dragon left, if some people have their will."

In the *Gentleman's Magazine* for March, 1788, a writer, on the authority of "a nobleman of the first consequence and information in this kingdom," makes the absurd statement that "*Robinson Crusoe* was written by the Earl of Oxford in the Tower,

and that he gave the manuscript to Daniel Defoe,
who frequently visited him during his confinement."

"Poor Ben" was perhaps Benjamin Tooke,
Swift's bookseller, to whose shop in the Middle
Temple Gate the Dean in 1718 directed two of his
letters to Chetwode. He brought out *The Tale of
a Tub*. There was another "Ben" known to Swift
—Benjamin Motte, the publisher of *Gulliver's
Travels*. Both men corresponded with him.

When the Dean writes, "we are here in horrible
fears," by "we" he means the Protestants. In
Ireland, when he speaks of "the nation," he always
means the English settlers. "The kingdom," he
wrote in 1726, "consists of a people who have a
claim of merit from their extraordinary loyalty to
the present King and his family." He describes
the inhabitants of Ireland as "a nation disowned by
their brethren and countrymen"—disowned, that is
to say, by the English of England. In all his writings it would not be easy to find a passage where
he shows any fellow-feeling for those whom he calls
"the poor Popish natives"; in this he was like
other Englishmen. "The English," he wrote,
"know little more of Ireland than they do of
Mexico; further than that it is a country subject
to the King of England, full of bogs, inhabited by
wild Irish papists, who are kept in awe by mer-
cenary troops; and their general opinion is, that it
were better for England if the whole island were
sunk into the sea." One hundred and fifty years

later, John Bright stated "the general opinion," not of the English but of the Irish, about this island : " I believe that if the majority of the people of Ireland, counted fairly out, had their will, and if they had the power, they would unmoor the island from its fastenings in the deep, and move it at least two thousand miles to the West."

The Archbishop of Dublin, in 1709, described the reversal of the outlawry of an Irish nobleman who had taken up arms for James II. in 1688, as causing "a universal consternation." Fifty years later the Lord Chancellor at a trial " made the famous declaration, that the law did not presume that an Irish Papist existed in the kingdom." Nevertheless, in 1727 the Primate Boulter had written : " There are probably in this kingdom five Papists at least to one Protestant." Even the Protestant Irish were slighted by Englishmen. To a friend who sent Swift an account of a "mayor squabble" in Dublin he wrote back from London, "We regard it as much here as if you sent us an account of your little son playing at cherry stones."

Five days after the date of Swift's letter the Pretender landed at Peterhead in Scotland. A few weeks later he fled back to France.

" My Friend Mr. Attorney" was perhaps the ex-Lord Chancellor Harcourt, who had been Attorney-General part of the time that Swift was writing his *Journal to Stella*. Erasmus Lewis wrote to Swift in 1714 : " The great attorney, who made you the

sham offer of the Yorkshire living, had a long conference with the dragon on Thursday, kissed him at
parting, and cursed him at night." In a note on
this passage in Scott's edition it is suggested that
Lord Chancellor Harcourt is meant.

The danger at this time of "conversation with
different principles" Swift recalled nine years later
in a sermon entitled *On Doing Good*, preached in
St. Patrick's. He says : "Neither is it long since
no man, whose opinions were thought to differ from
those in fashion, could safely converse beyond his
nearest friends, for fear of being sworn against as a
traitor, by those who made a traffic of perjury and
subornation ; by which the very peace of the nation
was disturbed, and men fled from each other as they
would from a lion or a bear got loose."

"Honest people" meant either Jacobites or, at
all events, Tories. When Dr. Panting, Master of
Pembroke College, Oxford, preached at St. Mary's
the sermon on the anniversary of the accession of
George I., Hearne wrote : "He is an honest gent.
His sermon took no notice, at most very little, of
the Duke of Brunswick." In like manner Hearne
described one Mr. How as "a famous cavalier,
and a very honest man."

Dr. Pr—— was probably Dr. Pratt, mentioned
post p. 106.

XVI.

[*To Knightley Chetwode Esqᵣ at Mr. Took's shop, at the Middle-Temple Gate in Fleetstreet. London.*]

DUBLIN. *Sept 2d* 1718.

I received your first of Aug 13ʰ when I was just leaving Galstown—from whence I went to a Visitation at Trim. I saw Dame. I stayd two days at Laracor, then 5 more at a Friends, and came thence to this Town, and was going to answer yᵣ Lett. [your Letter] when I received the 2ᵈ of Aug 23ᵈ. I find it is the opinion of yᵣ Friends that you should let it be known as publickly here as can be done, without overacting, that you are come to London, and intend soon for Ireland, and since you have sett [? let] Woodbrooke I am clearly of opinion that you should linger out some time at Trim, under the notion of staying some time in order to settle; you can be conveniently enough lodged there for a time, and live agreably and cheap enough, and pick up rent as you are able; but I am utterly opposite to your getting into a Figure all on a sudden, because every body must needs know that travelling would not but be very expensive to you, together with a scattered Family, and such conduct will be reckoned prudent and

discreet, especially in you whose Mind is not altogether suited to y^r Fortune. And therefore tho' I
have room enough in an empty Coach-house w^h
[which] is at y^r service yet I wish you would spare
the Expences, and in return you shall fill the Coach-
house with anything else you please.—I fear you
will return with great contempt for Irel^d where yet
we live tolerably quiet, and our enemyes seem to
let us alone mearly out of wearyness. It was not
my fault that I was not in Engl^d last June.—I
doubt you will make a very uneasy Change from
Dukes to Irish Squires and Parsons, wherein you
are less happy than I, who never loved great company, when it was most in my Power, and now I
hate every thing with a Title except my Books,
and even in those the shorter the Title the better
—And (you must begin on the other side for I
began this Letter the wrong Way) whenever you
talk to me of Regents or Grandees I will repay
you with Passages of Jack Grattan and Dan
Jackson. I am the onely man in this Kingdom
who is not a Politician, and therefore I onely keep
such Company as will suffer me to suspend their
Politicks and this brings my Conversation into very
narrow Bounds. Jo Beaumont is my Oracle for
publick Affairs in the Country, and an old Presbyterian Woman in Town. I am quite a Stranger

to all Schemes and have almost forgot the difference between Whig and Tory, and thus you will find me when you come over—Adieu. My true love to Ben—

Notes on XVI.

In the letter dated April 28, 1731, which I quote at the end of this book, published in Swift's works as addressed "To Ventoso," but written to Chetwode, though never sent, Swift says : "You went abroad, and strove to engage yourself in a desperate cause." He adds : "You are pleased that people should know you have been acquainted with persons of great names and titles." He hints, however, that all this talk of treason had been an invention of Chetwode's. There are passages in the present letter which seem to imply that Chetwode had been plotting among the Jacobites abroad. He had, we read, to make a "change from Dukes to Irish Squires and Parsons," and his talk was likely to run on "Regents or Grandees." He would have visited the Duke of Ormond, who by the help of a lady of great beauty, but easy morals, vainly hoped to win over the Duke of Orleans, Regent of France, to the Pretender's cause. He would have passed on to Spain, where Cardinal Alberoni, the prime minister, was scheming to send an armament to Scotland under Ormond's command. The fleet set sail, but it was shattered by a storm. Only two ships reached Scotland. More than fifty years later Johnson and Boswell visited the wild glen where the handful of Spaniards and their Highland allies were routed by General Wightman. In other quarters Alberoni's policy had failed. Chetwode had scarcely set foot in England when the news arrived of the sea-fight off Sicily between an English and a Spanish squadron, described by an English captain in the briefest of despatches: " Sir, we have taken and destroyed all the Spanish ships which were upon the coast ; the number as per margin."

" In Ireland," said Swift, "the neighbouring squires are usually the most disagreeable of all human creatures." To one of them who cheated him of his tithes he wrote : " Your faculty lies in making bargains ; stick to that. Leave your children a better estate than your father left you, as he left you much more than your grandfather left him. . . . One thing I desire you will be set right in ; I do not despise all squires. It is true . I despise the bulk of them. But pray take notice that a squire must have some merit before I shall honour him with my contempt, for I do not despise a fly, a maggot, or a mite."

In the following lines he expresses the contempt he felt not only for Irish squires, but also for Irish lords :—

" In exile with a steady heart
He spent his life's declining part ;

7

> Where folly, pride and faction sway,
> Remote from St. John, Pope and Gay.
> His friendships there to few confined
> Were always of the middling kind ;
> No fools of rank, a mongrel breed,
> Who fain would pass for lords indeed ;
> Where titles give no right or power,
> And peerage is a withered flower ;
> He would have held it a disgrace
> If such a wretch had known his face.
> On rural squires, that kingdom's bane,
> He vented oft his wrath in vain."

That he "never loved great company" even in London he thus boasts :—

> " He never thought an honour done him,
> Because a duke was proud to own him ;
> Would rather slip aside and choose
> To talk with wits in dirty shoes ;
> Despis'd the fools with stars and garters,
> So often seen caressing Chartres."

In spite of his boast, "there frequently appears in his letters," to quote Johnson's words, "an affectation of familiarity with the great." Thus he wrote to Stella: "The Duchess of Shrewsbury came up and reproached me for not dining with her. I said, that was not so soon done; for I expected more advances from ladies, especially duchesses." To the Duchess of Queensberry he wrote : "I am glad you know your duty; for it has been a known and established rule above twenty years in England, that the first advances have been constantly made by all ladies who aspired to my acquaintance, and the greater their quality, the greater were their advances." "I have a cloud of witnesses," he told Pope, "with my Lord Bolingbroke at their head, to prove I never practised or possessed such a talent as civility."

In his *Journal to Stella*, after mentioning the Duke and Duchess of Ormond and Lord-Treasurer Oxford, he continues : "Prithee, don't you observe how strangely I have changed my company and manner of living ? I never go to a coffee-house ; you hear no more of Addison, Steele, Henley, Lady Lucy, Mrs. Finch, Lord Somers, Lord Halifax &c. I think I have altered for the better."

The Rev. Daniel Jackson is introduced in the lines where Swift urges Delany to warn Dr. Sheridan against carrying jests too far :—

> "You must, although the point be nice,
> Bestow your friend some good advice ;
> One hint from you will set him right,
> And teach him how to be polite.
> Bid him, like you, observe with care,
> Whom to be hard on, whom to spare ;
> Nor indistinctly to suppose
> All subjects like Dan Jackson's nose."

When Swift says that he is not a politician, it is true of this period of his life. During almost six years after his return to Ireland he kept to his resolution of not meddling at all with public affairs. After the death of the Queen, to quote Johnson's words, "nothing remained but to withdraw from the implacability of triumphant whiggism, and shelter himself in unenvied obscurity."

The "old Presbyterian Woman," was Mrs. Brent, his housekeeper. "I have an elderly housekeeper," he wrote to Pope, "who has been my Walpole above thirty years, whenever I lived in this kingdom." In another letter he says, "I see no creature but my servants and my old Presbyterian housekeeper." "She is famous in print," he adds, "for digging out the great bottle." It was dug out to celebrate Stella's birthday in 1723, as described by the Dean in his verses on the day.

XVII.

[*To Knightley Chetwode Esqr to be left at Mr. Took's shop at the middle Temple gate in Fleet-street London.*]

DUBLIN. *Novr* 25. 1718.

I have had your Letters, but have been hindred from writing by the illness of my head, and eyes, which still afflict me. I have not been these five months in the Country, but the People from Trim tell me that yours are all well.

I do not apprehend much consequence from what you mention about Informations etc. I suppose it will fall to nothing by Time—You have been so long in the grand monde that you find it difficult to get out. I fear you mistook it for a Compliment, when you interpret something that I said as if you had a Spirit above your Fortune. I hardly know anybody but what has the same, and it is a more difficult Virtue to have a Spirit below our Fortune, which I am endeavouring as much as I can, and differ so far from you, that instead of conversing with Lords (if any Lord here would descend to converse with me) that I wholly shun them for People of my own Level, or below it, and I find Life much easyer by doing so ; but you are younger and see with other eyes. The Epigram you mention is but of two Lines. I have done with those Things. I desired a young Gentleman to paraphrase it, and I do not much like his Performance, but if he mends it I will send it to Ben, not to you—I think to go soon into the Country for some weeks for my Health, but not towards Trim I believe—Mr Percivall is dead and so is poor Parvisol. This is a bad Country to write news from. Ld Archibald Hamilton is going to be marryed to one Lady Hamilton the best match in this Kingdom—Remember me to Ben and John when you see them—Neither my Head nor Eyes will suffer me to write more, nor if they did have I anything materiall to add but that I am yr &c.

Notes on XVII.

In Swift's collected correspondence there is no letter between July 18, 1717, and May, 1719. He seems to have consulted Dr. Arbuthnot about the illness from which he was suffering, who on Dec. 11, 1718 sent him a prescription for his vertigo.

Mr. Percival lived at Laracor. "I can send you no news," wrote Swift from that place, "only the employment of my parishioners may, for memory-sake, be reduced under these heads: Mr. Percival is ditching; Mrs. Percival in her kitchen; Mr. Wesley switching; Mrs. Wesley stitching; Sir Arthur Langford *riching*, which is a new word for heaping up riches." The rest of the passage is too coarse to quote. Percival brought to Swift, in London, news of his plantations, "He tells me that the quicksets upon the flat in the garden do not grow so well as those famous ones on the ditch. They want digging about them. The cherry trees by the river side my heart is set upon."

"Poor Parvisol," an Irishman of French extraction, had been Swift's tithe-agent at Laracor. Of him he had written, four years earlier: "Such a rascal deserves nothing more than rigorous justice. He has imposed upon my easiness, and that is what I never will forgive. I beg you will not do the least thing in regard to him but merely for my interest, as if I were a Jew, and let who will censure me."

Lord Archibald Hamilton, son of the Duke of
Hamilton, married Lady Jane Hamilton, daughter
of the Earl of Abercorn. Their son, Sir William
Hamilton, was the husband of Lord Nelson's Lady
Hamilton. Lady Jane Hamilton became, it was
reported, the mistress of Frederick, Prince of
Wales.

XVIII.

*[To Knightley Chetwode Esqr at his House at
Woodbrooke near Portarlington.]*

DUBLIN. *Apr* 29*th* 1721.

S^R,—Your Servant brought your Lett^r when I
was abroad, and promised to come next morning at·
8 but never called : so I answer it by Post ; you·
have been horribly treated, but it is a common
Calamity. Do you remember a Passage in a Play
of Molière's Mais qu Diable avoit il à faire dans
cette Galere? What had you to do among such
company? I shew'd your Lettr yesterday to the
A. Bp. [Archbishop] as you desire : I mean I read
the greatest Part to him—He is of opinion you
should take the Oaths ; and then complain to the
Goverm^t [Government] if you thought fit. But I
believe neither—nor any body can expect you would
have much Satisfaction—considering how such complaints are usually received. For my own Part I

do not see any Law of God or Man forbidding us
to give security to the Powers that be : and private
men are not [to] trouble themselves about Titles to
Crowns, whatever may be their particular Opinions.
The Abjuration is understood as the Law stands ;
and as the Law stands, none has Title to the Crown
but the present Possessor ; By this Argument more
at length, I convinced a young Gentleman of great
Parts and Virtue ; and I think I could defend my
self by all the Duty of a Christian to take Oaths to
any Prince in Possession. For the word Lawfull,
means according to present Law in force ; and let
the Law change ever so often, I am to act according to Law ; provided it neither offends Faith nor
Morality : You will find a sickly man when you
come to Town ; and you will find all Partyes and
Persons out of humour ; I envy your Employm^ts
[Employments] of improving Bogs ; and yet I envy
few other Employments at present My humble
service to Mrs Chetwode and believe me to be,
ever, sincerely yours &c.

Notes on XVIII.

Swift was thinking of the passage in " Les Four-
beries de Scapin " where the father exclaims, " Que
diable allait-il faire dans cette galère ? " " I forsook
the world and French at the same time," the Dean

writes on December 5 of this year. His French seems to have forsaken him when he wrote " qu " for " que." According to John Forster, he was accomplished in French. Sir William Temple more justly said of him that " he has Latin and Greek, some French."

High Churchman though he was, he cared nothing for the divine right of kings. " I always declared myself," he wrote, "against a Popish successor to the crown, whatever title he might have by the proximity of blood : neither did I ever regard the right line except upon two accounts ; first, as it was established by law, and secondly as it has much weight in the opinions of the people. For necessity may abolish any law, but cannot alter the sentiments of the vulgar ; right of inheritance being perhaps the most popular of all topics ; and therefore in great changes, when that is broke, there will remain much heart-burning and discontent among the meaner people."

The nonjuror Hearne took a very different view of the oath of abjuration. " Notwithstanding its abominable wickedness," he wrote in 1723, "it is incredible what numbers of all kinds run in to swear." Three years later he recorded : " A Scottish man whispered me in the ear, 'You are the only honest man in Oxford. You want a larger gullet to swallow damned cramp oaths.'"

When Swift wrote to Chetwode, " I envy your Employm^{ts} of improving Bogs " this was no passing

caprice.   Into the mouth of the king of Brobdingnag
he put sentiments which he really felt, when he
made him say that "whoever could make two ears
of corn, or two blades of grass to grow upon a spot
of ground where only one grew before, would
deserve better of mankind, and do more essential
service to his country than the whole race of
politicians put together."   Arthur Young held with
Swift in this.   In his tour through Ireland in 1776
he made such entries as the following : " I saw two
large compost dunghills turning over and mixing, a
sight not common in Ireland.   It pleased me more
than the sight of a palace would have done."   " I
saw four men hoeing a field of turnips.   These were
the first turnip hoers I have seen in Ireland, and I
was more pleased than if I had seen four emperors."

XIX.

[Indorsed by Chetwode, "*upon ye Subject of my quarrell with Coll.—— at Maryborough Assizes.*"]

DUBLIN. *May* 9. 1721.

S^R,—I did not answer your last because I would
take time to consider it   I told the Ar. B^p what
you had done, that you had taken the Oathes &c.
and then I mentioned the Fact about Wall who
brought a Challenge &c. tho you did not tell from

whom : and whether you should apply to have him put out of the Commission ; the A. B^p said he thought you ought to let the matter rest a while, and when you have done so, and get your Materialls ready and that it appears not to be a sudden Heat, he did hope the Chancell^r would do you Justice.

As to the Business of Sandis going about for hands I know not what to say. That was rather a Scoundrell than an illegal Thing, and probably will be thought merit and zeal rather than a Fault ; I take your Part to be onely despising it; as you ought to do the Bravery of his Brother, and his manner of celebrating it ; For my own Part (and I do not say it as a Divine) there is nothing I have greater contempt for than what is usually stiled Bravery, which really consists in never giving just offence, and yet by a generall Demeanour make it appear that we do not want Courage, though our Hand is not every Hour at our Hilt—I believe your courage has never been suspected ; And before I knew you I had heard you were rather much too warm, and you may take what Sandis said, as a Compl^{mt} [Compliment] that his Brother's Bravery appeared by venturing to quarrell with you.

You are to know that few persons have less Credit with the present Powers than the A. B^p and therefore the Redress you are to expect must be from

the justice of those who have it in their way to do
you right ; I mean those at the Helm or rather who
have their little finger at the helm, which however is
enough for your use, if they will but apply it ; But
in great Matters of Governm^t the L^d L^t [Lord-
Lieutenant] does all, and these folks can not make a
Vicar or an ensign.

I am y^r &c.   J. S.

My humble Service to y^r Lady.

Notes on XIX.

The name of the colonel with whom Knightley
Chetwode quarreled I have omitted at the request of
the present owner of Woodbrooke.

According to the *New English Dictionary*
" bravery," in its first sense, was " the action
of braving or acting the bravo ; daring, defiance ;
boasting, swaggering ; bravado."

Thomas Sheridan, writing of Dublin a few years
earlier than the date of Swift's letter, says, " At that
time party ran very high, but raged no where with
such violence as in that city, insomuch that duels
were every day fought there on that score."

The Duke of Grafton, Lord-Lieutenant of Ireland,
two years later thus wrote of Archbishop King to
Sir Robert Walpole : " He is of as uncommon a
mixture as most people I know. He is very indiscreet in his actions and expressions, pretty ungovern-

able, and has some wild notions, which sometimes make him impracticable in business, and he is, to a ridiculous extent, national. Upon some points (of which the jurisdiction of the House of Lords is one) he loses both his temper and his reason." After adding that he had objected to the words "a happy people" in the Lord-Lieutenant's speech at the opening of Parliament, as "they were in some respect put under slavery," the Duke continued : "He is very well affected to the King, and an utter enemy to the Pretender and his cause. He is charitable, hospitable, a despiser of riches, and an excellent bishop."

XX.

[Indorsed, "*Swift dated at Dublin. June* 10 1721 *the A. Bishop's and his own opinion of the prosecution agst me.*"]

DUBLIN. *June* 10*th.* 1721.

S^R,—I received both your Letters and the Reason why I did not answer the first was because I thought I had said all I had to say upon the occasion, both as to the A. B^p's opinion and my own, but if that reason had not been sufficient there was another and a Better, or rather a Worse ffor I have been this last Fortnight as miserable as a Man can possibly be with an Ague, and after vomiting sweeting and Jesuits Bark, I got out to Day, but have been since my beginning to recover, so seized with a Daily Headake, that I am but a very scurvy recovered Man : I suppose you may write to the Chancell^r and tell him the full story, and leave the rest to him.

As to your Building I can onely advise you to ask advice, to go on slowly, and to have your House on Paper before you put it into Lime and Stone. I design in a very few Days to go somewhere into the Country, perhaps to Gallstown. I have been 7 years getting a Horse and have lost 100ᴵᴵ by buying without Success; Sheridan has got his Horses again—and I recovered one that my Servt had lost—Everybody can get Horses but I ; There is a Paper called Mist come out, just before May 29th terribly Severe : It is not here to be had ; the Printer was called before the Commons—it apply [? applied] Cromwell and his son to the present Court—White Roses we have heard nothing of to-day.

I am your most ob^{dt}   J. S.

My head is too ill to write or think.

NOTES ON XX.

The prosecution mentioned in Chetwode's indorsement was most likely connected with some

Jacobite plot. As will be seen in the letters written two years later he was again in dread of the government.

N. Mist was the printer of *The Weekly Jaurnal, or Saturday's Post, with Freshest Advices, Foreign and Domestic*. In the number for May 27, 1721, in an address beginning " Friends! Britons! Countrymen!" under cover of celebrating Restoration Day, an attack was made on the House of Hanover, and a fresh restoration of the Stuarts was advocated. In such a passage as the following it is easy to see that it was not Oliver and Richard Cromwell who were meant, but George I. and the Prince of Wales: " We groaned under the oppressive force of a cruel, ill-bred, uneducated Old Tyrant, and the drivelling fool his son, whilst the royal progeny wandered from court to court. The royal palace was crowded with trulls and scoundrels who would disgrace Bridewell and Newgate." The writer goes on to celebrate the benefit that followed " on the restoration of the monarchy in the Royal House of Stuart, in the person of a prince endowed with a thousand shining qualities. The College of Bishops was filled more worthily than in any age since the apostolical one. They were all Christians! pious, learned, orthodox confessors. Arts and sciences revived, joy diffused itself over every honest countenance, and gloomy dejected looks confined themselves to their proper district, the faces of rogues and villains. Learned judges were placed

upon the bench, who never enquired what the plain-
tiff or defendant was, but what was his cause. The
pulpits were rescued from nonsense and blasphemy.
St. Augustine, being asked what he would wish to
have seen of all that had been beheld by mortal man,
replied, 'Christ in the flesh, Paul in the pulpit, and
Rome in its glory.' Next to this wish, which is not
to be equalled in any proportion, I would desire to
see the Restoration. Upon it there was a universal
change from all that was wicked and detestable to all
that was good and desirable. But I may be asked,
Is this a time for joy when we labour under such
irretrievable calamities? Shall we return thanks
for a deliverance from rogues with swords in their
hands, when we are ruined by footmen, pimps,
parasites, bawds, harlots, nay what is more vexatious,
old ugly harlots! such as could not find entertainment in the most hospitable hundreds of old
Drury?"

The paper was voted "a false, malicious, scandalous, infamous and traitorous libel," and an
humble address was presented to the King assuring
him "that this House will stand by and support his
Majesty and his Royal Family against all traitorous
and seditious attempts that shall be made against his
sacred person and government." Mist was sent to
Newgate "to be kept in close custody." He was not
to be admitted the use of pen, ink, or paper. There,
no doubt, he was detained till August 10th, when the
House rose. Imprisonment in those days was a

dreadful punishment, unless for people who had money enough to pay for food and lodging. In one London gaol "a day seldom passed without a death; and upon the advancing of the spring, not less than eight or ten usually died every twenty-four hours." These facts are stated in the Report of a Committee of the House of Commons, which in 1729 examined the state of the gaols. No great improvement was made. In 1732 the Court of Common Council resolved that the place of Keeper of Newgate ought not to be sold. At the same meeting they voted "that the sum of £1000 should be given to the present Lord Mayor and Sheriffs as a proper satisfaction in lieu of the perquisites arising on the sale of the place." Eighteen years later more than twenty persons, who had attended the Sessions at the Old Bailey, died of fever. A list of them is given in the *Gentleman's Magazine* for May, 1750. In 1761 Wesley wrote: "Of all the seats of woe on this side hell few, I suppose, exceed, or even equal, Newgate."

Mist, undaunted, still published his paper, under the transparent disguise of *Fog's Journal*.

The white roses, of which Swift had heard nothing, were worn by the Jacobites, on June 10th, the day on which he was writing. It was the birthday of the Pretender. Addison, writing in *The Freeholder*, on June 22, 1716, says: "We have taken notice in former papers of this political ferment being got into the female sex, and of the

wild work it makes among them.   We have had a
late most remarkable instance of it in a contest
between a sister of the white rose, and a beautiful
and loyal young lady, who, to show her zeal for
Revolution principles, had adorned her pretty bosom
with a sweet william."   Swift mentions " the white
rosalists, tenth-a-junians and the like."   Churchill,
in his *Prophecy of Famine*, describes how in the
Highlands :—

> " Far as the eye could reach no tree was seen,
> Earth clad in russet scorn'd the lively green,
> The plague of locusts they secure defy,
> For in three hours a grasshopper must die.
>
> .   .   .   .   .
>
> No flowers embalm'd the air but one white rose,
> Which on the tenth of June by instinct blows,
> By instinct blows at morn, and when the shades
> Of drizzly eve prevail, by instinct fades."

Hearne records how on June 10, 1713, "they had
a terrible rackett with the Jacobite party at
Edinburgh.   The streets were crowded with all
sorts of people, huzzaing and hollowing, ' God save
the King, and down with Hanover and the whiggs !'
—playing and singing the old tune—

> " ' The King shall enjoy his owne again.' "

On June 11, 1726, the Primate Boulter wrote
from Dublin : " Yesterday in the evening a very
numerous rabble assembled in St. Stephen's Green,
as they usually have done on the 10th of June."

The soldiers were sent for, and firing with ball wounded three or four. " I do not find," the Primate continues, " that there was much more in it than the popish rabble coming down to fight the Whigg mob, as they used to do on that day."

XXI.

[Indorsed, "*a humorous pleast* [*pleasant*] *letter.*"]

GALSTOWN. *Septr* 14*th* 1721.

S^R,—I have been here these three months, and I either answered y^r former Letter, or else it required no answer. I left the Town on a sudden, and came here in a Stage Coach meerly for want of Horses. I intend a short Journey to Athlone, and some Parts about it, and then to return to Dublin by the end of this Month, when the weather will please to grow tolerable ; but it hath been so bad for these ten weeks past that I have been hindred from severall Rambles I intended. Yours of the 5 instant was sent here last Post ; It was easy for you to conceive I was gone out of Town considering my state of Health, and it is not my Talent to be un- kind or forgetfull, although it be my Misfortune as the World runs, to be very little Serviceable ; I was in hopes that y^r Affair by this time had come to some Issue, or at least, that you who are a warm

Gentleman, like others of your Temper, might have cooled by Degrees. For my own Part, I have learned to bear Every thing, and not to Sayl with the Wind in my Teeth. I think the Folke in Power, if they had any Justice, might at least give you some honorary Satisfaction : But I am a Stranger to their Justice and all their good Qualityes, having onely received Marks of their ill ones—

I had promised and intended a Visit to Will Pool, and from thence would have called at Woodbrook. But there was not a single Intervall of Weather for such an Expedition. I hope you have good Success with your Drains and other Improvements, and I think you will do well to imitate our Landlord here, who talks much of Building, but is as slow as possible in the Execution.

Mr Jervas is gone to Engl^d, but when I go to Town I shall Enquire how to write to him, and do what you desire ; I know not a more vexatious Dispute than that about Meres and Bounds, nor more vexatitious [*sic*] Disputants than those Righteous : I suppose upon the Strength of the Text, that the Righteous shall inherit the Land.

My humble Service to Your Lady.

I am your most humble &c.,

J. S.

JONATHAN SWIFT.
(By Charles Jervas.)

[To face page

Notes on XXI.

George Rochefort's house at Galstown, where Swift was staying, is thus described by Dr. Delany :—

> "'Tis so old and so ugly, and yet so convenient,
> You're sometimes in pleasure, though often in pain in't ;
> 'Tis so large, you may lodge a few friends with ease in't,
> You may turn and stretch at your length if you please in't ;
> 'Tis so little, the family live in a press in't,
> And poor Lady Betty has scarce room to dress in't ;
> 'Tis so cold in the winter, you can't bear to lie in't,
> And so hot in the summer, you are ready to fry in't ;
> 'Tis so brittle, 'twould scarce bear the weight of a tun,
> Yet so staunch that it keeps out a great deal of sun ;
> 'Tis so crazy, the weather with ease beats quite through it,
> And you're forced every year in some part to renew it ;
> 'Tis so ugly, so useful, so big, and so little,
> 'Tis so staunch and so crazy, so strong and so brittle,
> 'Tis at one time so hot, and another so cold,
> It is part of the new, and part of the old ;
> It is just half a blessing, and just half a curse—
> I wish then, dear George, it were better or worse."

Swift had come to Galstown, or Gaulstown, as early as July 5th of this year, as one of his letters to Vanessa shows. In it he says : "Cad [Cadenus] assures me he continues to esteem and love, and value you above all things, and so will do to the end of his life, but at the same time entreats that you would not make yourself or him unhappy by imaginations. The wisest men in all ages have thought it the best course to seize the minutes as they fly, and to make every innocent action an amusement. If you knew how I struggle for a little health, what uneasiness I am at in riding and walking, and refraining from everything agreeable to my taste, you would think it but a small thing to take a coach now and then, and converse with fools and impertinents, to avoid spleen and sickness." Then follows one of those passages which led Horace Walpole—rightly, I believe—to infer that the connection between Swift and Vanessa was a guilty one.[1]

A fortnight later than the date of Swift's letter to Chetwode he wrote to the Archbishop of Dublin : " I own my head and your grace's feet would be ill joined ; but give me your head and take my feet, and match us in the kingdom, if you can. My Lord, I row after health like a waterman, and ride after it like a postboy, and find some little success ; but subeunt morbi tristisque senectus. I have a receipt to which you are a stranger ; my Lord Oxford and Mr. Prior used to join with me in taking it ; to whom I often said, when we were two hours diverting ourselves with trifles, *vive la bagatelle*. I am so deep among the workmen at Rochefort's canals and lakes, so dexterous at the oar, such an alderman after the hare—"

In some lively verses entitled *The Country Life*, Swift bids—

---

[1] See Walpole's letter to George Montague, dated June 20, 1766.

" Thalia tell in sober lays,
How George,[1] Nim,[2] Dan,[3] Dean,[4] pass their days.

.   .   .   .   .

Begin my Muse ! First from our bowers
We sally forth at different hours ;
At seven the Dean, in night-gown [5] drest,
Goes round the house to wake the rest ;
At nine grave Nim and George facetious
Go to the Dean to read Lucretius ;
At ten my lady comes and hectors,
And kisses George, and ends our lectures ;
And when she has him by the neck fast,
Hauls him, and scolds us down to breakfast. '

They dined at two and supped some time after sunset.

The Dean decamped from his friend's house suddenly and secretly. On reaching home he wrote to Dan Jackson : " I fell upon a supposition that Mr. Rochefort had a mind to keep me longer, which I will allow in him and you, but not one of the family besides, who, I confess, had reason enough to be weary of a man who entered into none of their tastes, nor pleasures, nor fancies, nor opinions, nor talk. . . . You are now happy, and have nobody to teaze you to the oar or the saddle. You can sit in your night-gown till noon without any reproaches."

The " honorary Satisfaction " that might have been given to Chetwode was perhaps that English

---

[1] George Rochefort.   [2] John Rochefort, the Nimrod of the party.
[3] Rev. Daniel Jackson.   [4] Dean Swift.
[5] Dressing-gown. " A loose gown used for an undress."—*Johnson's Dictionary*.

peerage in claiming which his grandfather had ruined himself.

Mr. Jervas was Charles Jervas the painter, known also as the translator of *Don Quixote*, to whom Pope addressed an epistle. He painted a portrait of Swift in London, and another in Ireland. Gay described him as "robust and debonair." "Kneller remarked on hearing that he had set up a carriage and four horses : 'Ah, mine Cot, if his horses do not draw better than he does he will never get to his journey's end.'"

XXII.

DUBLIN. *Novr.* 11*th* 1721.

S^r,—I received yours yesterday. I writ to Mr Jervas from the Country, but have yet received no answer, nor do find that any one of his Friends hath yet heard from him, so that some of them are in a good deal of pain to know where he is, and whether he be alive. I intend however to write a second time, but I thought it was needless to trouble you till I could say something to the Purpose. But indeed I have had a much better or rather a much worse Excuse, having been almost three weeks pursued with a Noise in my Ears and Deafness that makes me an unsociable Creature, hating to see others, or be seen by my best Friends, and wholly confined to my Chamber—I have been often troubled with it but never so long as now, which wholly disconcerts and confounds me to a degree that I can neither think nor speak nor Act as I used to do, nor mind the least Business even of my own, which is an Apology I should be glad to be without. I am ever   Yr &c.

J. S.

Note on XXII.

The deafness of which Swift complains in this letter grew worse and worse, till at last it cut him off from all society. Five years before his death he wrote to his cousin: " I have been very miserable all night, and to-day extremely deaf and full of pain. I am so stupid and confounded that I cannot express the mortification I am under both in body and mind. All I can say is, that I am not in torture ; but I daily and hourly expect it. Pray let me know how your health is and your family. I hardly understand one word I write. I am sure my days will be very few ; few and miserable they must be.

" I am, for those days, yours entirely,

" Jon. Swift.

" If I do not blunder, it is Saturday, July 26, 1740.

" If I live till Monday I shall hope to see you, perhaps for the last time."

XXIII.

DUBLIN. *Decembr 5th* 1721.

S^R,—When I received your French Letter I was
going to write you an English one. I forsook the
World and French at the same time, and have
nothing to do with the Latter further than sometimes reading or gabbling with the French clergy
who come to me about business of their Church car
je parle à peindre, mais pour l'ecrire je n'en songe
guere depuis que j'ay quitté le politique. I am but
just recovered of my Deafness which put me out of
all Temper with my self and the rest of Mankind.
My Health is not worth a Rush nor consequently
the Remaining Part of my Life.

I just now hear that Dr Prat Dean of Down, my
old Acquaintance is dead, and I must here break off
to go to his Relations.

—9. The poor Dean dyed on Tuesday, and was
buried yesterday, he was one of the oldest Acquaintance I had, and the last that I expected to dy. He
has left a young Widow, in very good Circumstances.
He had Scheems of long life, hiring a Town-house,
and building a Countrey, preparing great Equipages
and Furniture. What a ridiculous Thing is Man—
I am this moment inevitably stoppt this moment
[*sic*] by company, and cannot send my Letter till
next Post.

—12. I have writ twice to Mr Jervas, and got no
Answer, nor do I hear that any one has ; I will
write again when I can be informed where to reach
him ; you hear the Bank was kicked out with
Ignominy last Saturday—This Subject filled the
Town with Pamphlets and none writt so well as by
Mr Rowley though he was not thought to have
many Talents for an Author.   As to my own Part,
I mind little what is doing out of my proper
Dominions, the Libertyes of the Deanery ; yet I
thought a Bank ought to be established, and would
be so because it was the onely ruinous Thing, wanting to the Kingdom, and therefore I had not the
least Doubt but the Parlm^t would pass it.

I hope you are grown regular in your Plantations,
and have got some skill to know where and what
Trees to place, and how to make them grow.   For
want of better I have been planting Elms in the
Deanery Garden, and what is worse, in the Cathe-
drall Churchyard where I disturbed the Dead, and
angered the Living, by removing Tomb stones,
that People will be at a Loss how to rest with the
Bones of their Ancestors.

I envy all you that lived retired out of a world
where we expect nothing but Plague, Poverty, and
Famine which are bad words to end a Letter with ;
therefore with wishing Prosperity to you and your
Family, I bid you Adieu.

NOTES ON XXIII.

" The French clergy " belonged to the Huguenot congregation, which met for worship in the Lady Chapel of St. Patrick's Cathedral. The use of it, writes W. M. Mason in his *History of St. Patrick's*, had been granted them in 1663 ; "in 1816 the Chapel was resumed, the congregation having become extinct. In June, 1689, the minister and several members of the congregation were seized and delivered to the Count D'Avaux, in order to be sent over to France. Through the mediation of friends they obtained a respite, and by the overthrow of the papal power at the Boyne a final release from the execution of this cruel sentence." In 1766 there were in Dublin, we are told, "three churches for French, and one for Dutch Protestants."

Seven years after the date of this letter Swift wrote to Pope : " You say, ' I am to blame if I refuse the opportunity of going with my Lady Bolingbroke to Aix la Chapelle.' I must tell you, that a foreign language is mortal to a deaf man. I must have good ears to catch up the words of so nimble a tongued race as the French, having been a dozen years without conversing among them."

Dr. Pratt had been Provost of Trinity College, Dublin. He had been a Tory ; but, as Swift said, " from a resolution of keeping as fair as he possibly could with the present powers" he had chosen the Prince of Wales Chancellor of the University. In the *Speech of the Provost of Trinity College to his Royal Highness the Prince of Wales*, Swift makes him say :—

> "Illustrious Prince, we're come before ye,
> Who, more than in our founders, glory
>   To be by you protected ;
> Deign to descend and give us laws,
> For we are converts to your cause,
>   From this day well-affected.
>
> Urged by a passionate desire
> Of being raised a little higher,
>   From lazy cloistered life ;
> We cannot flatter you, nor fawn,
> But fain would honoured be with lawn,
>   And settled by a wife." [1]

The Dean, however, had all along befriended Pratt, and had done what he could to get him promotion ; partly, perhaps, as not thinking him fit for the post he held. "I find," he wrote to the Archbishop of Dublin, "since he cannot be trusted with a bishopric, that he desires to leave his station with as good a grace as he can ; and that it may not be thought that what he shall get is only to get rid of him."

In his letter of July 19, 1725, Swift again repeats "how ridiculous a creature is man." As he grew older he spoke of his fellow-men more harshly. "I hate and detest that animal called man," he wrote.

---

[1] "The statutes of the University enjoined celibacy."

"It is a creature (taking a vast majority) that I hate more than a toad, a viper, a wasp, a stork, a fox, or any other that you will please to add." In this he was unlike Edmund Burke, who said: "From the experience which I have had—and I have had a great deal—I have learnt to think better of mankind."

By the "Bank" which "was kicked out with ignominy," Swift means the bill to establish a National Bank in Ireland—"a thing they call a bank" as he elsewhere spoke of it. "Bankrupts," he wrote to the Archbishop, "are always for setting up banks; how then can you think a bank will fail of a majority in both Houses?" A broadside, in which he examined the published list of subscribers, thus concludes:—

"N.B.—The total of men, women and children in Ireland, besides Frenchmen, is 2,000,000. Total of the land of Ireland, acres 16,800,000.

"Quære. How many of the said acres are in possession of 1 French baron, 1 French dean, 1 French curate, 1 French alderman, 10 French merchants, 8 Messieurs Frances, 1 esquire projector, 1 esquire attorney, and 6 officers of the army, 8 women, 1 London merchant, 1 Cork merchant, 1 Belfast merchant, 18 merchants whose places of abode are not mentioned, 1 cashier, 4 bankers, 1 gentleman projector, 1 player, 1 chemist, 1 Popish vintner, 1 bricklayer, 1 chandler, 4 doctors of physic, 2 chirurgeons, 1 pewterer, 4 gentlemen attorneys, besides 28 gentlemen dealers, yet unknown, ut supra?" In a second tract he added to the list: "One French corn-cutter, one French drawer, one Deal merchant, one French apothecary, one Anabaptist clothier, one barrack-master, one butcher, and one agent's clerk, besides several South-Seaers and Mississippians." The South Sea Bubble had burst, and the Mississippi scheme had collapsed a year earlier.

"I have often wished," he wrote, "that a law were enacted to hang up half a dozen bankers every year, and thereby interpose at least some short delay to the farther ruin of Ireland." A little before the date of this letter he thus described a banker in the Day of Judgment:—

> " How will the caitiff wretch be scared,
>   When first he finds himself awake
> At the last trumpet, unprepared,
>   And all his grand account to make !
>
> When other hands the scales shall hold,
>   And he in men's and angels' sight
> Produced with all his bills and gold,
>   Weighed in the balance and found light."

These lines would have quite a modern ring were they carved on the walls of the church lately built " To the glory of God and in memory of Jay Gould."

Writing of his jurisdiction as Dean of St. Patrick's Swift says : " The Dean holds a court-leet in his district, and is exempt from the Lord Mayor &c." To Lord Castle Durrow he wrote on December 24,

1736: " My Housekeeper, a grave elderly woman, is called at home and in the neighbourhood Sr Robert. My Butler is Secretary, and has no other defect for that office but that he cannot write ; Yet that is not singular, for I have known three Secretarys of State upon the same level, and who were too old to mend, which mine is not. My realm extends to 120 Houses, whose inhabitants constitute the Bulk of my Subjects ; my Grand Jury is my House of Commons, and my Chapter the House of Lords. I must proceed no further, because my Arts of Governing are Secrets of State."

His cousin, Deane Swift, said that " Dr. Swift used to call the people who lived in the Liberty of St. Patrick's his subjects ; and, without dispute, they would have fought up to their knees in blood for him." When Sergeant Bettesworth threatened him with violence, above thirty of the inhabitants of the Liberty, " in the Name of themselves and the rest of their Neighbourhood," about the end of December, 1733, presented to him a paper, in which, after stating that " a certain Man of this City hath openly sworn by the Help of several Ruffians to murder or maim the Reverend the Dean of St. Patrick's, our Neighbour, Benefactor, and Head of the Liberty of St. Patrick's," they continued : " We do unanimously declare that from our great Love and Respect to the said Dean, we will defend the Life and Limbs of the said Dean against the said Man, and all his Ruffians and Murderers, as far as the Law doth allow."

Swift, who was ill in bed, dictated to them an answer in which he spoke "of the great Amity in which the inhabitants of the Liberty, as those of the Neighbourhood," had lived with him " for near twenty Years." According to Sir Walter Scott, he "returned the deputation thanks for their zeal, but enjoined them to disperse peaceably, and, adding a donation of two or three guineas, prohibited them from getting drunk with the money, adding, ' You are my subjects, and I expect you will obey me.' " Nevertheless in another place Scott, without noticing any absurdity, quotes Hawkesworth's statement that the deputation was composed of " thirty of the nobility and gentry of St. Patrick's." Hawkesworth's blunder arose from his carelessly reading the account of this affair given in the *Gentleman's Magazine* for January, 1734.

The Liberty contained five acres and a half.

A year after the date of this letter Swift wrote to a friend : " You never saw anything so fine as my new Dublin plantations of elms ; I wish you would come and visit them." Neither in the Deanery garden nor in the cathedral churchyard has a single tree survived of all those he planted.

XXIV.

[Indorsed, "*a very droll and pleast letter.*"]

DUBLIN. Jany 30*th* 1721–2.

S^R,—I have been these five weeks and still continue so disordered with a Noise in my Ears and Deafness that I am utterly unqualifyed for all Conversation or thinking. I used to be free of these Fits in a fortnight but now the Disease I fear is deeper rooted, and I never Stir out, or Suffer any to See me but Trebbles and countertennors, and those as Seldom as possible.

I have often thought that a Gentleman in the Country is not a bit less happy for not having Power in it, and that an Influence at Sizes and Sessions, and the like, is altogether below a wise man's Regard, especially in such a dirty obscure nook of the World as this Kingdom. If they break open your Roads, they cannot hinder you from going through them. You are a King over your own District though the neighboring Princes be your Enemyes ; you can pound the Cattle that trespass on your Grounds, tho' the next Justice replevins them : you are thought to be quarrelsom enough and therefore peacefull people will be less fond of provoking you. I do not value Bussy's maxim of Life, without the Circumstances of Health and

Money :—Your Horse is neither Whig nor Tory, but will carry you safe unless he Stumbles or be foundered—By the way, I am as much at a loss for one as ever, and so I fear shall continue till my riding days are over.

I should not much mislike a Presentment against your going on with your House, because I am a mortal Enemy to Lime—and Stone, but I hope yours moves slowly upwards.

We are now preparing for the Plague, which every body expects before May; I have bespoke two pair of Shoes extraord^{ry}. Every body else hoards up their Money, and those who have none now, will have none. Our great Tradesmen break, and go off by Dozens, among the rest Archdeacon Bargons Son.

Mr Jervas writes me Word, that Morris Dun is a Person he has turned off his Lands, as one that has been his constant Enemy &c, and in short gives him such a Character as none can be fond of. So that I believe you were not apprized on what foot that Man stands with Mr Jervas.—I am quite weary of my own Ears, so with Prayers for you and your Fire Side,

I remain y^r &c.

Notes on XXIV.

" The Trebbles and countertennors " were people whose voices he could hear, as is shown by the following passages in his letters : " When the deafness comes on I can hear with neither ear, except it be a woman with a treble and a man with a counter-tenor." " This deafness unqualifies me for all company, except a few friends with counter-tenor voices, whom I can call names if they do not speak loud enough for my ears." " I sometimes receive one or two friends and a female cousin, with strong, high, tenor voices."

Sir Roger de Coverley did not share Swift's contempt of " an Influence at Sizes and Sessions." The *Spectator* tells us how, at an assize, " the court was sat before Sir Roger came ; but notwithstanding all the justices had taken their places upon the bench, they made room for the old knight at the head of them ; who for his reputation in the country took occasion to whisper in the judge's ear that he was glad his lordship had met with so much good weather in his circuit."

How much Ireland was regarded as an " obscure nook of the World " is shown by Pope when he writes to Swift : " I look upon a friend in Ireland as upon a friend in the other world, whom (popishly speaking) I believe constantly well-disposed towards me, and ready to do me all the good he can in that state of separation." Swift himself constantly abused the country in which he was born. "You all live," he wrote, "in a wretched, dirty doghole and prison, but it is a place good enough to die in." "I am become an obscure exile in a most obscure and enslaved country. . . . I would prefer living among the Hottentots, if it were in my power."

How much an Irish squire was "King over his own district" Arthur Young showed fifty-four years later. "A landlord in Ireland," he wrote, "can scarcely invent an order which a servant, labourer, or cottar dares to refuse to execute. Nothing satisfies him but an unlimited submission. Disrespect, or anything tending towards sauciness, he may punish with his cane or his horsewhip with the most perfect security. . . . It must strike the most careless traveller to see whole strings of cars whipt into a ditch by a gentleman's footman to make way for his carriage."

"Bussy Rabutin," writes Swift, "the politest person of his age, when he was recalled to Court after a long banishment, appeared ridiculous there." His maxim of life was no doubt contained in his *Discours à ses enfants sur le bon usage des adversitez.*

Swift showed that he was "an Enemy to Lime and Stone" when he wrote to a friend who was building: "I reckon you are now deep in mire and mortar, and are preparing to live seven years hence." Johnson was astonished that his friend, Dr. Taylor, should begin to build in his old age,

"and should condemn part of his remaining life to
pass among ruins and rubbish."

Swift, "who was nervously apprehensive of infectious diseases," had written to Stella from London
in 1710: "We are terribly afraid of the plague;
they say it is at Newcastle. I begged Mr. Harley,
for the love of God, to take some care about it, or
we are all ruined. You remember I have been
afraid these two years." In 1720 it had devastated
Marseilles. Pope celebrated the devotion of the
bishop :—

> "Why drew Marseilles' good bishop purer breath,
>   When nature sickened, and each gale was death?"

The bishop's devotion, however, increased the
mischief, for he gathered the people in crowds into
the churches, and scared them with the Day of
Judgment. Ramicus, Bishop of Arusiens in Dacia,
in his *Regimen contra Epidimiam siue Pestem*, had
shown far greater wisdom. This little treatise was
translated into English early in the sixteenth century, under the title of *A passing gode lityll Boke
necessarye and behouefull azenst the Pestilence*.
Among other remedies, cleanliness, constant wash-
ings, and temperance are strictly enjoined, and the
good bishop, well knowing how much the well-
being of the body depends upon the ease of the
mind, tells his patients that " to be mery in the herte
is a grete remedie for helth of the body; therefore
in time of this grete infirmite beware ye drede not

death, but lyue merely and hope to lyue longe."
At Oxford there had been talk about the spread of
the pestilence. Hearne recorded on January 21,
1720-1 : "I have been told that in the last great
plague at London none that kept tobacconists' shops
had the plague. I remember that I heard formerly
Tom Rogers, who was yeoman beadle, say, that
when he was that year, when it raged, a schoolboy
at Eaton ; all the boys of that school were obliged
to smoak in the school every morning, and that he
was never whipped so much in his life as he was
one morning for not smoaking." Whipping in times
of plague was not confined to schoolboys. By an
act of James I., "if any person infected with the
plague, or dwelling in any infected house, being
commanded by the mayor or constable to keep his
house, goes abroad and converses in company, if he
has no plague sore upon him, he shall be punished
as a vagabond by whipping ; but if he has any infectious sore upon him uncured, he then shall be
guilty of felony."

Under the dread of the plague spreading from
Marseilles an Act was passed by the English Parliament in 1721 for the building of pest-houses, to
which not only the infected, but even the healthy
members of an infected family were to be removed.
Round every town or city visited by the plague lines
were to be drawn which no one was to pass. In
vain it was objected that "two hundred thousand
men would not be sufficient to guard such great

cities as London and Westminster." A clause was added "impowering the King to order his officers to fire upon and sink any ship coming from an infected place." Happily the British Isles escaped the visitation. "The two pair of Shoes extraord^{ry}" which Swift bespoke were, no doubt, by way of preparation for the worst. If the plague came he would do his best to preserve his health by exercise. Twelve years later he wrote to a London merchant: "Oppressed beggars are always knaves; and I believe there hardly are any other among us. They had rather gain a shilling by knavery than five pounds by honest dealing. They lost £30,000 a year for ever in the time of the plague at Marseilles, when the Spaniards would have bought all their linen from Ireland; but the merchants and the weavers sent over such abominable linen, that it was all returned back, or sold for a fourth part of the value."

XXV.

[Indorsed, "*a very merry pleast letter.*"]

DUBLIN. *Mar* 13*th* 1721-2.

SIR,—I had a letter from you some time ago, when I was in no Condition for any Correspondence or Conversation; But I thank God for some time past I am pretty well recovered, and am able to hear my Friends without danger of putting

them into Consumptions. My Remedy was given me
by my Tayler, who had been four years deaf, and
cured himself as I have done, by a Clove of Gar-
lick Steeped in Honey, and put into his Ear, for
wch I gave him half a Crown after it had cost me 5
or 6 Pounds in Drugs and Doctors to no Purpose—
Surely you in the Country have got the London
Fancy, that I am Author of all the Scurvy Things
that come out here ; the Slovenly Pages called the
Benefit of—— was writt by one Dobbs a Surgeon.
Mr Sheridan sometimes entertains the World and I
pay for all. So that they have a Miscellany of my
works in England, whereof you and I are equally
Authors. But I lay all those Things at the Back
of my Book, which swells so much, that I am hardly
able to write any thing on the Forepart. I think
we are got off the Plague, tho I hear an Act of
Parl^{mt} was read in Churches (not in mine) concerning it, and the Wise say, we are in more danger
than ever, because infected Goods are more likely
to be brought us. For my Part, I have the Courage
of a Coward, never to think of Dangers till they
arrive, and then I shall begin to squeak. The
Whigs are grown such disaffected People that I
dare not converse with them ; and who your Britton
Esqr is, I cannot tell. I hear there is an Irish Paper
called the Reformer. I saw part of one Paper, but

it did not encourage me to enquire after more : I
keep the fewest Company of any man in this Town,
and read nothing that hath been written on this Side
1500 Years ; So you may judge what an Intelligencer I am like to be to a Gentleman in the
Country, who wants to know how the World goes.

Thus much for your first Letter, your last which
came just now is a Condolence on my Deafness.
M^r Le brunt was right in my Intentions, if it had
continued, but the Effect is removed with the
Cause. My Friends shall see me while I am neither
troublesome to them nor my self. I was less
melancholy than I thought I should have been,
and less curious to know what people said, when
they talked before me ; but I saw very few, and
suffered hardly any to stay :—People whisper here
too, just as they have whispered these 30 years, and
to as little Purpose.

I have the best Servant in the World dying in
the House, which quite disconcerts me. He was
the first good one I ever had, and I am sure will be
the last. I know few greater Losses in Life. I
know not how little you may make of Stone walls, I
am onely going to dash one in the Garden, and
think I shall be undone.

I hope y^r Lady and Fire side are well.

I am ever &c.

Notes on XXV.

Swift, it is said, only once directly owned any piece of writing as his. An Irish bishop, speaking to him of a new pamphlet, said that Burnet was the author. "When Swift seemed to doubt Burnet's right to the work, he was told by the bishop that he was 'a young man'; and, still persisting to doubt, that he was 'a very positive young man.' 'Then pray,' said the bishop, 'who writ it?' Swift answered, 'My Lord, I writ it.' It is to be supposed," adds Sheridan, " that the confession was drawn from him by the heat of the argument." He often complained that pieces were attributed to him which he had never written. " Since I left England," he wrote, "such a parcel of trash has been there fathered upon me, that nothing but the good judgment of my friends could hinder them from thinking me the greatest dunce alive." "Not a few of these alleged productions," writes Mr. Forster, "have found their way into his collected writings by the carelessness of his editors. Anything in the shape of a pun or indecency it was long the fashion to father on him without the least regard to either truth or probability."

So early as 1711 Swift wrote to Stella: "That villain Curll has scraped up some trash, and calls it Dr. Swift's Miscellanies, with the name at large, and I can get no satisfaction of him." A volume of his writings published a little earlier, was genuine, and had, it seems probable, his approval. " Tooke," he wrote, "is going on with my Miscellany." It was brought out by Morphew. " Some bookseller," he continued, "has raked up everything I writ and published it t'other day in one volume ; but I know nothing of it ; 'twas without my knowledge or consent ; it makes a four shilling book, and is called Miscellanies in Prose and Verse. Tooke pretends he know nothing of it, but I doubt he is at the bottom. One must have patience with these things ; the best of it is, I shall be plagued no more. However I'll bring a couple of them over with me for M.D. [Stella and her friend], perhaps you may desire to see them. I hear they sell mightily."

Before the beginning of the eighteenth century, according to Bishop Burnet, "the only division in Ireland was that of English and Irish, Protestants and Papists ; but of late an animosity came to be raised there like that we labour under in England, between Whig and Tory." Of the terms " Whig and Tory," he says : " I have spoken much against them, and even hated them ; but I must use them, they being now become as common as if they had been words of our language."

Swift, writing to Pope about the Irish Whigs, said : " I was discoursing some years ago with a certain minister about that Whiggish, or fanatical genius, so prevalent among the English of this Kingdom ; his lordship accounted for it by that number of

Cromwell's soldiers, adventurers, established here, who were all of the sourest leaven and the meanest birth, and whose posterity are now in possession of their lands and their principles."

His faithful servant, Alexander Magee, died within a few days. The Dean buried him in the cathedral, and read the service over him with tears in his eyes. Four and twenty years later, when his own turn came, and he was to be laid in the grave, his cousin, Mrs. Whiteway, indignant at "the sordid and unbecoming obscurity" in which the executors proposed to perform the funeral, wrote to one of them as follows : " Surely to hang the room Dr. Swift lies in with black, to give him an hearse, and a few mourning coaches, would be judged a funeral sufficiently private for so great a man ; and that he himself thought decency requisite at a funeral, may be known by what he did for his honest, trusty servant, Alexander Magee." Swift put over him the following inscription :—

> " Here lieth the body of
> Alexander Magee, servant to Doctor
> Swift, Dean of St. Patrick's.
> His grateful master caused this monument to be
> erected in memory of his discretion, fidelity,
> and diligence in that humble station.
> Ob. Mar. 24, 1721. Etat. 29."

" In the original draught," writes Dr. Delany,

" which I saw in the Dean's own handwriting, it stood thus :—

'His grateful *friend* and master, &c.'

A gentleman of the Dean's acquaintance, much more distinguished for vanity than wisdom, prevailed upon him to leave out the word '*friend*,' and only write 'his grateful master '; and this in contradiction to a known maxim of his own : 'That an affectionate and faithful servant should always be considered in the character of an humble friend.'" Lord Chesterfield held with him in this, who in his will, bequeathing legacies to all his household servants that had lived with him five years, added : "Whom I consider as unfortunate friends, my equals by nature, and my inferiors only by the difference of our fortunes."

Mrs. Pilkington tells how " Swift discharged a servant only for rejecting the petition of a poor old woman. She was very ancient, and on a cold morning sat at the Deanery steps a considerable time, during which the Dean saw her through a window. His footman happened to come to the door; and the poor creature besought him in a piteous tone to give that paper to his reverence. The servant read it, and told her with infinite scorn, ' His master had something else to mind than her petition.' 'What is that you say, fellow?' said the Dean, looking out at the window. 'Come up here.' The man tremblingly obeyed him. He also desired the poor woman to come before him, made her sit down, and ordered her some bread and wine. After which he turned to the man, and said, 'At what time, Sir, did I order you to open a paper directed to me, or to refuse a letter from any one? Hark ye, sirrah, you have been admonished by me for drunkenness, idling and other faults; but since I have discovered your inhuman disposition, I must dismiss you from my service, so pull off my clothes, take your wages, and let me hear no more of you.' The fellow did so, and having vainly solicited a discharge [a character], was compelled to go to sea, where he continued five years. At the end he begged the Dean would give him some sort of discharge, since the honour of having lived with him would certainly procure him a place." Swift gave him the following certificate :—

"DEANERY-HOUSE. *Jan.* 9. 1739-40.

"Whereas the bearer served me the space of one year, during which time he was an idler and a drunkard, I then discharged him as such; but how far his having been five years at sea may have mended his manners I leave to the penetration of those who may hereafter choose to employ him.

"JON. SWIFT."

Mrs. Pilkington adds that the man went to London, and was taken by Pope into his service, "in which he continued till the death of his master."

XXVI.

DUBLIN. *Feb.* 12*th* 1722–3.

Sᴿ,—Upon my Return last October, after five months absence in the Country, I found a Letter of yours, which I believe was then 2 months old ; it contained no Business that I remember, and being then out of Health and Humer, I did not think an Answer worth your Receiving ; I had no other Letter from you till last Friday, which I could not answer on Saturday, that being a day when the Bishop saw no Company ; however I was with him a few minutes in the Morning about signing a Lease and then I had onely time to say a little of your Business, which he did not seem much to enter into, but thought you had no Reason to Stir in it, and that you ought to stay till you are attacked, which I believe you never will be upon so foolish an Accusation. On Sunday when I usually see him, he was abroad against his Custom, and yesterday engaged in Business and Company. To-day he sees no body it being one of the two days in the week that he shuts himself up. I look upon the Whig Party to be a little colder in the Business of Prosecutions, than they formerly were, nor will they readily trouble a Gentleman who lyes quiet and minds onely his Gardens and Improvements. The Improbability of your Accusers Story will never let it pass, and the Judges have [having] been so often shamed by such Rascals, are not so greedy at swallowing Informations. I am here in all their Teeth which they have shewn often enough, and do no more. And the Ch. Just. [Chief Justice] who was as venomous as a Serpent was forced to consent that a noli prosequi should pass after he had layd his hand on his Heart in open Court and Sworn, that I designed to bring in the Pretender.

Do you find that your Trees thrive and your drained Bog gets a new Coat? I know nothing so well worth the Enquiry of an honest Man, as times run. I am as busy in my little Spot of a Town Garden, as ever I was in the grand monde; and if it were five or ten miles from Dublin I doubt I should be as constant a Country Gentleman as you. I wish you good success in your Improvements for as to Politicks I have long forsworn them. I am sometimes concerned for Persons, because they are my Friends, but for Things never, because they are desperate; I always expect to-morrow will be worse, but I enjoy today as well as I can. This is my Philosophy, and I think ought to be yours; I desire my humble Service to M^{rs} [*sic*] and am very sincerely

Your most obedient

humble Servt

J. S.

Notes on XXVI.

On February 22 Swift sent the following letter to Archbishop King :—

"DEANERY-HOUSE, *February* 22 1722–3.

"My Lord,—Mr. Chetwode intends to deliver in a petition to the government to-day, and entreated me to speak to your grace before he delivered it, which not having an opportunity to do, I make bold to enclose this letter, which your grace may please to read, and is the substance of what he desired me to say.

"I am, My Lord, with the greatest respect,

"Your grace's most dutiful,

"and most humble servant

"JON. SWIFT."

In a note on Nichols's edition of Swift's Works this petition is said to be about "Chetwode's very good pretensions to an English peerage, for which he presented several memorials ; but to no purpose."

Knightley Chetwode, it is probable, as has been shown in my notes on an earlier letter, had taken part in a Jacobite plot. The Pretender, in spite of the failure of two risings in Scotland, was still buoyed up with hope. In the autumn of 1722, in a foolish manifesto, he called upon George I. to give up to him the throne of his fathers, and undertook in return to acknowledge him as King, instead of Elector of Hanover. By the order of the two Houses of Parliament it was burnt before the Royal Exchange by the common hangman as a false, insolent and traitorous libel. The Habeas Corpus Act was suspended for a year, and many arrests were made. One man was hanged at Tyburn for high treason, and Atterbury, Bishop of Rochester, was banished. Chetwode was threatened with prosecution, as the next letter and the seven following show. In Letter XXXI. there is mention of a second petition, presented nearly a year later.

Swift had published in 1720 *A Proposal for the Universal Use of Irish Manufacture*, in which he mentions "the pleasant observation of somebody's, that Ireland would never be happy till a law were made for burning everything that came from England, except their people and their coals." He adds that "some ministers were apt from their high elevation to look down upon this kingdom, as if it had been one of their colonies of outcasts in America." He attacks the Irish landlords, "who by unmeasurable screwing and racking their tenants all over the kingdom have already reduced the miserable people to a worse condition than the peasants in France, or the vassals in Germany and Poland." After accusing these same landlords of attacking the bishops, he continues : " I know not how it comes to pass (and yet perhaps I know well enough) that slaves have a natural disposition to be tyrants, and that when my betters give me a kick, I am apt to revenge it with six upon my footman ; although perhaps he may be an honest and diligent fellow." The government, not being able to reach the author for want of proof, prosecuted the printer. " The jury," wrote Swift, "brought him in not guilty, although they had been culled with the utmost industry. The Chief Justice sent them back nine times and kept them eleven hours. During the trial, among other singularities, he laid his hand on his breast, and protested solemnly that the author's design was to bring in the Pretender, although there was not a single syllable of party in the whole treatise." Swift retaliated with satire. Among the bitter verses he wrote on this unjust judge the following are perhaps the bitterest :—

> " In church your grandsire cut his throat ;
> To do the job too long he tarried ;
> He should have had my hearty vote
> To cut his throat before he married."

The Dean in his lines *On the death of Dr. Swift* described the Chief Justice as :—

> " A wicked monster on the bench,
> Whose fury blood could never quench ;

As vile and profligate a villain
As modern Scroggs, or old Tresilian;
Who long all justice has discarded
Nor fear'd he God, nor man regarded."

The Earl of Chesterfield, when he was Lord-Lieutenant, favoured Irish manufactures. Mrs. Delany wrote from Dublin on Dec. 21, 1745: "Every-body is to appear at the Castle on the Prince of Wales's birthday in Irish stuffs, as they did on the Princess's."

The concern that Swift sometimes felt for persons, because they were his friends, he thus expressed in a letter to Pope: "I have ever hated all nations, professions and communities; and all my love is towards individuals; for instance, I hate the tribe of lawyers, but I love Counsellor Such-a-one and Judge Such-a-one. It is so with physicians (I will not speak of my own trade), soldiers, English, Scotch, French and the rest. But principally I hate and detest that animal called man; although I heartily love John, Peter, Thomas, and so forth." Of the letters that passed between him and Pope, Johnson said:—"They show the age involved in darkness, and shade the picture with sullen emulation."

XXVII.

S^R,—I was yesterday with A. B [Archbishop], who tells me that it was not thought fit to hinder the Law from proceeding in the common form, but that particular Instructions were given that you should be treated with all possible Favor; and I have some very good Reasons to believe those Instructions will be observed : neither in this do I speak by Chance : which is all I can say—I am y^{rs} &c.

Feb 25th 1722-3.
Monday Morn.

NOTE ON XXVII.

Archbishop King would know what was intended about the prosecution, as he was one of the Lords Justices. Evelyn, eighteen years earlier, had described him as "a sharp ready man in politics, as well as very learned."

XXVIII.

[To Knightley Chetwode Esq at his Lodgings in William Street :]

S^{R},—I sent a Messenger on Friday to Mr Forbes's Lodging, who had orders if he were not at home, to say that I should be glad to see him—but I did not hear of him, though I stayd at home on Saturday till past two a Clock. I think all y^{r} Comfort lyes in your Innocence, your Steddyness, and the Advice of y^r Lawyers. I am forced to leave the Town sooner than I expected.

I heartily wish you good Success, and am in hopes the Consequence will not be so formidable as you are apt to fear. You will find that Brutes are not to be too much provoked; they that most deserve Contempt are most angry at being contemned; I know it by Experience. It is worse to need Friends, than not to have them. Especially in Times when it is so hard, even for cautious men to keep out of harms way.

I hope when this Affair is over you will make y^r self more happy in y^r Domestick : that you may pass the rest of y^r Life in emproving the Scene and y^r Fortune, and exchanging y^r Enemyes for Friends.

I am &c.

June 2nd 1723.

Past twelve at night.

NOTE ON XXVIII.

Swift's use of the term "domestick" can be paralleled by the following quotation from the writings of his master, Sir William Temple :—"I was resolved to pass the rest of my Life in my own Domestick, without troubling myself further about any publick Affairs."

XXIX.

[Indorsed, " *Swift without date abt my Prosecution and his sentiments on severall particulars abt it. K. C.*"]

S^R,—I was just going out when I received y^r note ; these proceedings make my head turn round ; I take it that the Governments leave for you to move the King's Bench must signify something, or else instead of a Dilemma it is an Absurdity. I thought you had put in a Memoriall, which I also thought would have an Answer in form. I apprehend they have a mind to evade a Request which they cannot well refuse ; will not y^r lawyer advise you to move the King's Bench ? and will he not say that it was the Direction of the Government you should do so ? and will the Government own an advice or order that is evasive ? I talk out of my Sphere. Surely the Attorney cannot reconcile this. I imagined y^r request should [have] been offered to the Justices in a Body not to one and then to t'other, which was doing nothing. I am wholly at a Loss what to say further.

XXX.

S^R,—I sd [said] all I possibly could to D^r C—— and it is your Part to cultivate it, and desire that he

will make the A. B. soften the Judge—you want
some strong credit with the L^t [Lord-Lieutenant]
or proper methods with those under him—As to
putting you off, till the L^t goes ; I think that can do
no hurt. I suppose it is impossible for the Parl^t
[Parliament] to rise till after Christmas, since they
are now begining Bills that will pass with Difficulty, and if there be an Indemnity, then there will
be an End. I believe all people agree with you,
that y^r concern shocks you more than it does others.
I am sure I saw my best friends very calm and easy
when I was under worse difficultyes than you. A
few good offices is all we can expect from others.

Notes on XXX.

Dr. C—— was probably the same man as Dr.
Cog^l of Letter XXXII., who was Marmaduke
Coghill, LL.D. " A cause was brought before
him as Judge of the Prerogative Court, wherein a
man was sued for beating his wife. The Doctor
gave his opinion, that 'although a man had no
right to beat his wife unmercifully, yet with such a
little cane or switch as he then held in his hand,
a husband was invested with a power to give his
wife moderate correction.' This opinion determined the lady to whom he was to have been
shortly married against having him. He died an
old man and a bachelor."

" The Irish Parliament was only called together every second year. The session usually began in October, and ended in the following March or April, during which short period there were always one or two long adjournments."

The calmness and easiness of Swift's friends when he was under difficulties can be justified by Johnson's reflection that " life occupies us all too much to leave us room for any care of others beyond what duty enjoins; and no duty enjoins sorrow or anxiety that is at once troublesome and useless."

It was perhaps his " best friends " that Swift had in mind when he wrote :—

> " In all distresses of our friends
> We first consult our private ends ;
> While Nature kindly bent to ease us
> Points out some circumstance to please us."

His false friends he goes on to attack in the following lines :—

> " By innocence and resolution
> He bore continual persecution ;
> While numbers to preferment rose
> Whose merits were to be his foes ;
> When ev'n his own familiar friends,
> Intent upon their private ends,
> Like renegadoes now he feels
> Against him lifting up their heels."

XXXI.

S^r,—I endeavrd once or twice without Success to see the B^p [Bishop] he was so taken up with the Delegates. But it is no great matter. I met an intimate Friend of his yesterday, a considerable, who told me, that the Bishop took y^r Affair to heart, and would attend the Ld. L^t [Lord-Lieutenant] with y^r Petition, and take the Sollic^r Gen [Solicitor-General] with him, and the Person who told me these was equally concerned for you, and as I believed he would see the B^p before me, I pressed him again. He s^d the L^d L^t he believed went to Pearsby's[1] yesterday, but would return in a Day or two.

I am so much out of order that I could not go to Church, and shall have a mixt company with me to-night, so that I can not encourage you to be among them.

I am &c.

Jany 19.

1723 4

Notes on XXXI.

There is no example in the *New English Dictionary* of "considerable" as a noun used of a

[1] This word is not clear in the original.

person, though there are examples of it used of a thing.

In the Dublin State Paper Office, as I learn from the kindness of the Keeper, Dr. J. J. Digges La Touche, is a copy of an extract of a letter from the Duke of Newcastle to the Lord-Lieutenant, dated April 14, 1724, stating that his Majesty, on the petition of Knightley Chetwode and two others, has given orders for putting a stop to the prosecutions against them.

XXXII.

[Indorsed, " *Upon no great business.*"]

S^r,—I see nothing wrong in the petition if your friends are satisfied in relation to that part where you mention the Differences you have with Gentlemen in the country, but others can advise you in that better. I spoke with the Bp. of C—— and Dr. Cog^l as much as I could think of tother day, and the latter particularly who s^d he would do all he could, and said it heartily, as did the other. I went abroad yesterday directly fm [from] Church, and to-day is the busiest day I have in the year, so that I have hardly time to write this or to think. To-morrow will be likewise a day of business, however, if it be for y^r service I will to-morrow aftern. find an hour to talk with you. I wish you good Success and am &c.   Thursday.

NOTES ON XXXII.

The Bishop of C—— was probably the Bishop of Clogher, with whom Swift was on friendly terms. Perhaps the Bishop of Cork was meant, of whom Swift wrote to Sheridan a year later: "If you are under him, he is a capricious gentleman; but you must flatter him monstrously upon his learning and his writings; that you have read his book against Toland a hundred times, and his sermons (if he has printed any) have been always your model, &c."

Dr. Cog^l was Dr. Coghill.

XXXIII.

S^r,—I had not y^r lett^r [letter] till I returned home and if I had I could not have known what to do. I think you should have attended the Bishop, and pressed him to what I desired in my letter, for I could not speak more urgently nor could I am able [*sic*] to say much more with him than what I wrote. Mr Bernard is a favorite of the Times and might have credit with the Attor^y Genl [Attorney-General] to agree that the Thing should be granted, but he lyes still, and onely leaves you to do that which he can better do himself. I w^d [would] do six times more than you desire even for a perfect stranger, if he were in Distress, but I have turned the Matt^r [Matter] a thousand times in my Thoughts in vain. I believe y^r wisest friends will think as I do, that the best way will be to move the Sec^{try} [Secretary] in that manner he likes best—I am this moment going to Prayers and so remain y^{rs} &c.

Thursday mor. 9 o'clock.

NOTES ON XXXIII.

Mr. Bernard was perhaps Francis Bernard, who in 1713 was Solicitor-General.

"The manner to move the Secretary" of the Lord-Lieutenant "which he liked best" was probably a bribe. By a bribe so applied by a brother clergyman Swift twenty-four years earlier had lost the rich deanery of Derry. The Lord-Lieutenant of that day, the Earl of Berkeley, had promised him "the first good preferment that should fall in his gift." When Derry fell vacant, and Swift asked for it, "the Earl said that 'Bush [his secretary] had been beforehand with him, and had got the promise of it for another.' Upon seeing Swift's indignation rise at this, my Lord, who began to be in no small fear of him, said, 'that the matter might still be settled, if he would talk with Bush.' Swift immediately found out the Secretary, who very frankly told him that he was to get a thousand pounds for it, and, if he would lay down the money, he should have the preference.   To which Swift, enraged to the utmost degree at an offer which he considered as the highest insult, and done evidently with Lord Berkeley's participation, made no other answer but this : ' God confound you both for a couple of scoundrels!'   With these words he immediately quitted the room, and turned his back on the Castle, determined to appear there no more. But Lord Berkeley was too fearful of the resentment of an exasperated genius.   He therefore immediately presented him with the rectory of Agher, and the vicarages of Laracor and Rathbeggan."

XXXIV.

DUBLIN. *Jul.* 14*th* 1724.

S^R,—I had yours of Jun 27th and have been hindred by a great variety of Silly Business and Vexation from answering you.   I am over head and ears in Mortar—and with a number of the greatest Rogues in Irel^d [Ireland] which is a proud word ; But besides I am at an uncertainty what to say to you on the Affair you mention : what new Reason you may have, or discoverys you have made of foul Play I cannot but be a stranger to. All I know is, that any one who talked of y^r

Prosecution while you were here, unanimously condemned it as villanous and unjust, which hath made me think that it would be better to lye in oblivion, for my Reason of agreeing formerly that an Account of it would be usefull, went onely on the Supposition, that you would be tryed &c. But I protest I am no fit Adviser in this matter, and therefore I would entreat you to consult other Friends, as I would do if it were my own case. If you are advised to go on and pursue that Advice, by drawing up the Account, pray do it in Folio, with the Margin as wide as the writing, and I shall add alter or correct according to my best Judgment and though you may not be advised to publish it, yet it may be some Amusement in wet winter Evenings. I hope you found y^r Plantations answer what you expected. You will hear that the Primate dyed yesterday at twelve o'Clock which will set the expecting Clergy all in a motion : and they say that Leving the Chief Justice dyed about the same Hour, but whether the Primate's death swallows up the other I cannot tell ; for either it is false or not regarded ; perhaps I shall know before this is closed. Ld [Lord] Oxford dyed like a great man, received visits to the last, and then 2 minutes before his Death, turned from his Friends, closed his own Eyes, and expired: Mr Stopford is returned from his Travells, the same Person he went, onely more experience; he is the most in all regards the most valuable young Man of this Kingdom.

I am ever &c.

Leving is dead.

Notes on XXXIV.

Swift was "over head and ears in Mortar" in building a wall round a plot of ground, to which he gave the name of "Naboth's Vineyard." According to Mrs. Pilkington, speaking of it to her, he said he "had cheated one of his neighbours out of it." She continues: "When they entered the garden, or rather the field, which was square, and enclosed with a stone wall, he asked her how she liked it. 'Why, pray, Sir,' said she, 'where is the garden?' 'Look behind you,' said he. She did so, and observed the south wall was lined with brick, and a great number of fruit trees planted against it, which, being then in blossom, looked very beautiful. 'What are you so intent on?' said the Dean. 'The opening bloom,' replied she, which brought Waller's lines to her remembrance—

"'Hope waits upon the flow'ry prime.'

'Oh!' replied he, 'you are in a poetical vein; I

11

thought you had been taking notice of my wall.
It is the best in Ireland.   When the masons were
building it (as most tradesmen are rogues), I
watched them very close, and as often as they
could they put in a rotten stone, of which, however, I took no notice until they had built three
or four perches beyond it.   Now, as I am an
absolute monarch in the liberties [of St. Patrick's],
and King of the rabble, my way with them was
to have the wall thrown down to the place where
I observed the rotten stone ; and by doing so five
or six times, the workmen were at last convinced
it was their interest to be honest."   This severity,
it is interesting to know, was not without good
result.   I learn by an article in the *Irish Builder*
for May, 1897, that "all the stone wall lined on
the outside with brick is still standing, and the
brick is in good preservation."

" ' Naboth's garden ' continued to be annexed to
the Deanery until the year 1814, when the ground
was sold for the purpose of erecting an hospital
[the Meath Hospital] thereon."

The Primate of Ireland was Lindsay, Archbishop
of Armagh.   Writing to Swift some years earlier,
he had quoted Archbishop Tillotson's remark,
"that if he should hearken to what the Irish
clergy said of one another, there was not a man
in the whole country that ought to be preferred."
The Dean himself wrote in 1725 :—" I heard King
William say that if the people of Ireland could be

believed in what they said of each other, there was not an honest man in the Kingdom." On hearing of the Primate's death, Swift wrote at once to the Archbishop of Dublin, urging him to accept the primacy if it were offered to him, "because I would have your name left to posterity among the primates; and because entering into a new station is entering, after a sort, on a new lease of life; and because it might be hoped that your grace would be advised with about a successor." He was passed over on account of his age. When the new Primate, Dr. Boulter, called on him, he received him without rising from his chair. "'My Lord,' said he, 'I am certain your Grace will forgive me, because you know I am too old to rise.'"

It was in memory of Boulter that Dr. Madden twenty years later wrote a poem which he gave Johnson ten guineas to correct. It contained such lines as the following:—

"Ha! mark! what gleam is that which paints the air?
The blue serene expands! Is Boulter there?"

Swift's scorn of the bishops of the Irish Church is shown in the lines where, in the person of St. Patrick addressing Ireland, he likens them to magpies sent

"from the British soil
With restless beak thy blooming fruit to spoil;
To din thine ears with unharmonious clack,
And haunt thy holy walls in white and black."

In another poem, writing of them, he says :—

> " Of whom there are but four at most
> Who know there is a Holy Ghost ;
> The rest, who boast they have conferr'd it,
> Like Paul's Ephesians, never heard it ;
> And when they gave it, well 'tis known,
> They gave what never was their own."

To one of them he wrote : " It is happy for me that I know the persons of very few bishops ; and it is my constant rule never to look into a coach, by which I avoid the terror that such a sight would strike me with."

In 1710 he described to Stella a dinner given at Skinner's Hall in London by the Londonderry Society, at which the Chief Justice was present. " Three great tables with the desert laid in mighty figure. Sir Richard Levinge and I got discreetly to the head of the second table, to avoid the crowd at the first ; but it was so cold, and so confounded a noise with the trumpets and hautboys, that I grew weary, and stole away before the second course came on, so I can give you no account of it, which is a thousand pities."

The Earl of Oxford died on May 21. Hearne recorded on June 28th that " he died in a very quiet, composed manner, and that he put his hand up, and closed his own eyes and fixed his jaw." Swift wished to write his life. " I have already taken care," he had written to him a few years earlier, " that you shall be represented to posterity as the ablest and faithfullest minister, and truest lover of your country that this age has produced." Posterity has formed its own judgment, and looks on his lordship as a shifty, pitiful creature. His colleague, Lord Chancellor Cowper, wrote of him, " His humour is to love tricks when not necessary, but from an inward satisfaction in applauding his own cunning."

" The most valuable young Man of this Kingdom," whom Swift thus put before Berkeley, became a bishop. Laurence Sterne was a boy of eleven. Burke and Goldsmith were not yet born.

XXXV.

S[r],—I have been above 7 weeks ill of my old Deafness and am but just recovered. Y[r] Carrier has behaved himself very honorably, because you took Care to seal the Cords. Y[r] Bergamot Pears are excellent, and the Orange Bergamots much best [*sic*] than those about this Town. Your Apples are very fair and good of their kind, and y[r] Peaches and Nectarines as good as we could expect from the Year. But it is too great a Journy for such nice Fruit, and they are apt to take the Tast of the Moss. Y[r] Cherry Brandy I depend on the goodness of, but would not suffer it to be tasted till another Time. I could find Fault with nothing but y^r Paper, which was so perfumed that the Company with me could not bear it.

There is a Draper very popular, but what is that to me——If Woods be disappointed it is all we desire.

Ld : Carteret is coming suddenly over.

I am y^r &c.

Notes on XXXV.

On September 3, 1724, Swift wrote to Lord Carteret : " I have been this month past so pestered with the return of a noise and deafness in my ears, that I had not spirit to perform the common offices of life, much less to write to your excellency."

The Irish carrier of Swift's day was on the same level of honesty as the conductors on the Italian railways of our time, against whose thievings the prudent traveller guards himself by cording his portmanteau and sealing the cord.

The "Draper" was the third of a series of letters signed "M. B. Drapier" by which Swift roused the Irish against the reception of a new copper currency. "What I did for this country," he wrote some years later, "was from perfect hatred of tyranny and oppression, for which I had a proclamation against me of £300, which my old friend, my Lord Carteret, was forced to consent to, the very first or second night of his arrival hither. The crime was that of writing against a project of one Wood, an iron-

A

LETTER

TO THE

Shop Keepers, *Tradesmen,* *Farmers,*
and *Common-People* of *IRELAND,*

Concerning the

Brass Half-Pence

.Coined by

Mr. 𝕮𝖆𝖔𝖔𝖉𝖘,

WITH

A **DESIGN** to have them Pass in this
K I N G D O M.

Wherein is shewn the Power of the said PATENT
the Value of the HALF-PENCE, and how far every Person
may be oblig'd to take the same in Payments, and how
to behave in Case such an Attempt shou'd be made by
WOODS or any other Person.

[Very Proper to be kept in every FAMILY.]

By M. B. Drapier.

Dublin : Printed by *J. Harding* in *Molesworth's-*
Court.

monger, to coin £100,000 in halfpence, not worth a sixth part of the money, which was laid before the people in so plain a manner that they all refused it ; and so the nation was preserved from immediate ruin." In another letter, speaking of his "foolish zeal in endeavouring to save this wretched island," he continues : " I have in twenty years drawn above one thousand scurrilous libels on myself, without any other recompense than the love of the Irish vulgar, and two or three dozen signposts of the Drapier in this city, besides those that are scattered in country towns ; and even these are half worn out."

He did not stick at a lie or two in his Drapier Letters. The English halfpence, he says, were of such good metal that a brasier would not lose much more than a penny in a shilling if he beat them to pieces and used them as copper. Whereas " Mr. Wood made his halfpence of such base metal, and so much smaller than the English ones, that the brasier would not give you above a penny of good money for a shilling of his." The assay of Sir Isaac Newton, who was Master of the Mint, proved the grossness of the exaggeration. There was little need of lying, for the job which Swift exposed was scandalous enough in itself. The King's mistress, the Duchess of Kendal, was to receive £10,000 from Wood as a bribe for the grant of the patent. This does not prove, however, that the new currency would not have been a great improvement on the old.

In the first *Drapier's Letter* Swift miscalls the patentee Woods, as he miscalls him in writing to Chetwode. In later *Letters* the error is corrected.

Lord Carteret was coming over as Lord-Lieutenant. Swift once had a dispute with him about the grievances of Ireland. "Carteret replied with a mastery and strength of reasoning, which Swift, not well liking, cried out in a violent passion : 'What the vengeance brought you among us? Get you back, get you back. Pray God Almighty send us our boobies again.'" In some verses written a few years later the Dean describes him as not one of those

> "Who owe their virtues to their stations,
> And characters to dedications."

He concludes—

> "I do the most that friendship can,
> I hate the viceroy, love the man."

"As for futurity," Carteret wrote to him, "I know your name will be remembered when the names of Kings, Lord-Lieutenants, Archbishops, and Parliament politicians will be forgotten." In another letter he said : "When people ask me how I governed Ireland, I say that I pleased Dr. Swift.

> "' Quæsitam meritis sume superbiam.' "

Plain. We are at a great Diſtance from the *King's Court*, and have no body there to ſolicite for us, although a great Number of *Lords* and *Squires*, whoſe Eſtates are here, and are our Country-men, ſpending all their *Lives* and *Fortunes* there. But this ſame Mr. VVOODS was able to attend conſtantly for his own Intereſt ; he is an ENGLISH MAN and had GREAT FRIENDS, and it ſeems knew very well *where to give Money*, to thoſe that would ſpeak to OTHERS that could ſpeak to the KING and could tell A FAIR STORY. And HIS MA-JESTY, and perhaps the great Lord or Lords who adviſed him, might think it was for our *Country's Good* ; and ſo, as the Lawyers ex-preſs it, the KING was deceived in his Grant, which often happens in *all Reigns*. And I am ſure if his MAJESTY knew that ſuch a Patent, if it ſhould take-Effect according to the Deſire of Mr. VVOODS, would utterly Ruin this Kingdom which hath given ſuch great Proofs of it's *Loyalty* he would immediately recall it, and perhaps ſhew his Diſpleaſure to SOME BODY OR OTHER, *But a Word to the Wiſe is enough*. Moſt of you muſt have heard with what Anger our *Honourable Houſe of Commons* received an Account of this VVOODS's PA-TENT. There were ſeveral *Fine Speeches* made upon it, and plain Proofs that it was all A VVICKED CHEAT from the *Bottom to the Top*, and ſeveral *Smart Votes* were printed, which that ſame VVOODS had the aſſurance to an-ſwer likewiſe in *Print*, and in ſo confident a

A 3   Way

n

That Carteret deceived either Swift or the English Government seems clear from his despatch quoted *post* page 181.

XXXVI.

[Indorsed, "*About H. C. ye Method of Parting, question of Allowance, Stopford and other materiall difficulties.*"]

DUBLIN, *Octr* 1724.

S^R,—I received your longer Letter, and afterwards your shorter by Mr Jackman. I am now relapsed into my old Disease of Deafness, which so confounds my Head, that I am ill qualifyed for writing or thinking. I sent your Letter sealed to Mr Stopford. He never showed me any Letter of y^{rs} nor talked of anything relating to you above once in his Life and that was some years ago, and so of [*sic*] little consequence that I have forgot it, and therefore I sent your letter sealed to him by a common Messenger only under the Inspection of a discreet Servant. I have lived in good Friendship with him, but not in such an Intimacy as to interfere in his Business of any sort, and I am sure I should not be fond of it unless I could be of Service —As to what you mention of my Proposall at the Deanery, as far as a confused Head will

give me leave to think; I was always of opinion
that those who are sure they cannot live well together, could not do a better thing than to part.
But the Quantum of y^r Allowance must be measured
by your Income and other Circumstances.   I am of
opinion that this might be best done by knowing
fairly, what the Person her self would think the
lowest that would be sufficient for what you propose,
and the Conditions of the Place to reside in, wherein
if you disapprove, you have Liberty to refuse, and in
this Mr Stopford's Mediation would be most convenient.   I desire you will give some Allowance to
his Grief and Trouble in this Matter.   I solemnly
protest he hath not mentioned one Syllable of this
to me, and if he should begin, I think I would inter-
rupt him—It is a hard Thing to convince others of
our Opinion, and I need not tell you how far a
Brother may be led by his Affections.   I am likewise of Opinion that such a thing as Parting, if it
be agreed on, may be done without Noise, as if it
were onely going to visit a Friend, and the Absence
may continue by degrees, and little notice taken.
As to the Affair of your Son, I can not imagine why
Mr Stopford hath not answered y^r Letter; I do
believe there is some what in that Business of his
Amour, an Affair begun in much youth, and kept up
perhaps more out of Decency and Truth than

Prudence. But he is too wise to think of proceeding further before he gets into some Settlem[t]
[Settlement] which may not probably be in severall
Years, and I prefer him as a Tutor absolutely before
any of his Age or Standing at least. The Discipline
in Oxford is more remiss than here—and since you
design he shall live in this Kingdom (where M[r] Jack-
mans tells me you are preparing so fine a Habitation
for him) I think it better to habituate him to the
Country where he must pass his Life, especially
since many chargeable accidents have happened to
you (besides your Building) which will press parsi-
mony upon you, and 50[li] a year will maintain your
Son a Commoner on which Conditions you will
place him, if you intend he shall be good for Something.

You will allow for this confussed Paper for I have
the noise of seven Watermills in my Ears and expect
to continue so above a Month, but this sudden Return
hath quite discouraged me. I mope at home and
can bear no Company but Trebles and counter-
teners.

I am ever &c.

Your Perfumed Paper hath been ready to give me
an Apoplexy either leave off these Refinements or
we will send you to live on a mountain in Connaught.

Notes on XXXVI.

So strong a disagreement had risen between Chetwode and his wife—the " Dame Plyant " of earlier letters, the mistress of that " little fire-side " to which Swift used to send kind messages·—that they were thinking of separating.   Stopford, as this letter shows, was her brother.   He was at this time a Fellow of Trinity College, Dublin.   The " amour which he had begun in much youth " was evidently innocent, " kept up " as it was, " perhaps more out of decency and truth than prudence."   By marriage he would have forfeited his fellowship.   The settlement to which he could look forward was preferment in the Church.   Lord Carteret gave him a vicarage.   Mrs. Delany wrote in 1753 :   " Dr. Berkeley's bishopric is bestowed on a very learned, ingenious good man, Dr. Stopford, who has been in expectation of one for twenty years past."

The discipline of Oxford from the Restoration onwards kept sinking and sinking, till it reached its lowest depth of degradation toward the close of the eighteenth century. Swift, it is reported, once asked a young clergyman if he smoked. " Being answered that he did not, ' It is a sign,' said he, ' you were not bred in the University of Oxford, for drinking and smoking are the first rudiments of learning taught there ; and in these two arts no university in Europe can outdo them.' "   Nevertheless, in his Essay on Modern Education he says that though he " could add some hundred examples from his own observation of men who learnt nothing more at Oxford than to drink ale and smoke tobacco," there were others who made good use of their time there, " and were ready to celebrate and defend that course of education." In his *Essay on the Fates of Clergymen* he thus describes the course of an Oxford student who was destined to rise high in the Church : " He was never absent from prayers or lecture, nor once out of his college after Tom [the great Christ Church bell] tolled. He spent every day ten hours in his closet, in reading his courses, dozing, clipping papers, or darning his stockings ; which last he performed to admiration. He could be soberly drunk at the expense of others with college ale, and at those seasons was always most devout. He wore the same gown five years without dragling or tearing. He never once looked into a playbook or a poem. He never understood a jest or had the least conception of wit." A Fellowship at Dublin "differed" as Swift pointed out, " in some very important circumstances from most of those in either of the Universities in England. It is obtained with great difficulty by the number of candidates, the strict examination in many branches of learning, and the regularity of life and manners."

There were, however, two sides to the picture. Hearne, writing at Oxford nineteen years before the date of Swift's letter, speaks ill of the Irish university. " The library of Trinity coll. in Dublin, where the noble study of Bishop Usher was placed, is quite neglected, and in no order, so that 'tis perfectly useless; the provost and fellows of that coll. having no regard for books and learning." Towards the end of last century the library was only opened "from eight to ten in the morning and from eleven to one at noon," while "no person was suffered under any pretence to take books away." On holidays it was closed. In Christ Church, Oxford, the discipline does not seem to have been remiss under Dean Aldrich, who died in 1710. Hearne tells us that "he rose to five o'clock prayers in the morning, summer and winter, visited the chambers of young gentlemen, on purpose to see that they employed their time in useful and commendable studies. He was a severe student himself, yet always free, open and facetious." On the other hand Lord Chesterfield, writing to Dr. Madden in 1749, about the University of Dublin, said: "Our two universities will do it no hurt, unless by their examples; for I cannot believe that their present reputations will invite people in Ireland to send their sons there. The one (Cambridge) is sunk into the lowest obscurity; and the existence of Oxford would not be known, if it were not for the treasonable spirit publicly avowed, and often exerted there. The University of Dublin has this great advantage over ours; it is one compact body under the eye and authority of one head, who, if he be a good one, can enforce order and discipline, and establish the public exercises as he thinks proper." R. L. Edgeworth, who in 1761 entered Trinity College, Dublin, as a fellow-commoner, says that "it was not the fashion in those days to plague fellow-commoners with lectures." He mentions his "total neglect of study," and adds "my father prudently removed me from Dublin to Oxford. Having entered Corpus Christi College, I applied assiduously not only to my studies under my excellent tutor, Mr. Russell, but also to the perusal of the best English writers, both in prose and verse." Russell was father of the Master of the Charterhouse whom Thackeray has celebrated in *Pendennis*.

XXXVII.

[Indorsed, "*About James Stopford, and placing my son Vall: under his care in Coledge of Dublin.*"]

DUBLIN. *Decr* 19*th* 1724.

S^R,—The Fault of my Eyes the Confusion of my Deafness and Giddyness of my Head have made me commit a great Blunder. I am just come from the Country where I was about 3 weeks in hopes to recover my Health; thither y^r last Letter was sent me, with the two inclosed, Mr Stopford's to you and yours to him. In reading them, I mistook and thought y^{rs} to him had been onely a Copy of what

you had already sent to him so I burned them both
as containing Things between y'selves, but I preserved y^{rs} to me to answer it, and now reading it
again since my Return, I find my unlucky Error,
which I hope you will excuse on Account of my
many Infirmityes in Body and Mind.   I very much
approve of putting y^r Son under Mr Stopford's Care,
and I am confident you need not apprehend his
leaving the College for some years, or if he should,
care may be taken to put the young Lad into good
Hands, particularly under M King—I am utterly
against his being a Gentleman Commoner on other
Regards besides the Expence : and I believe 50^{ll} a
Year (which is no small sum to a Builder) will
maintain him very well a creditable Pensioner.   I
have not seen the L^t [Lord-Lieutenant] yet, being
not in a Condition to converse with any Body, for
want of better Ears, and better Health—I suppose
you do not want Correspondents who send you the
Papers Current of late in Prose and Verses on
Woods, the *Juryes*, the Drapier &c.   I think there
is now a sort of Calm, except a very few of the
lowest Grubstreet but there have been at least a
Dozen worth reading—And I hope you approve of
the grand Juryes Proceedings, and hardly thought
such a Spirit could ever rise over this whole
Kingdom.   I am &c.

NOTES ON XXXVII.

Swift, in writing of a gentleman commoner, is applying to Dublin the term with which he had become familiar during his short residence in Oxford. The fellow commoner and pensioner of Dublin correspond to the gentleman commoner and commoner of the English university.[1] The gentleman commoner, whose showy gown was often seen in Oxford in my undergraduate days, is as extinct as the dodo. So late as 1833 they still numbered one hundred and fifty. "In Dublin," as I am informed on high authority, "any one who chooses to pay his money foolishly can be a fellow commoner. He sits at the fellows' table and is distinguished by some points of college costume. Above him in rank is the son of a peer." It was as a gentleman commoner that Gibbon, about thirty years after the date of Swift's letter, entered Magdalen College, Oxford. He dined with the fellows and was privileged to share in their "dull and deep potations," and to join in their conversation "as it stagnated in a round of college business, Tory politics, personal anecdotes, and private scandal." At Christ Church, Oxford, in 1769, "the expense of a commoner keeping the best company was near £200 a year; that of a gentleman commoner at least £250." At other

[1] In Worcester College, Oxford, the term "fellow commoner" was used.

colleges a commoner could have lived in decent comfort on £100.

Of the verses on Wood many were written by Swift—some of them brutal enough. The following epigram is inoffensive :—

> "Carteret was welcom'd to the shore
> First with the brazen cannons' roar ;
> To meet him next the soldier comes,
> With brazen trumps and brazen drums ;
> Approaching near the town he hears
> The brazen bells salute his ears :
> But when Wood's brass began to sound,
> Guns, trumpets, drums and bells were drown'd."

The grand jury, having thrown out the bill against the printer of the *Drapier's Letters*, was discharged by the chief justice in a rage. A new one was summoned, which made a presentment drawn up by Swift against "the base metal coined, commonly called Wood's half-pence," of which they "had already felt the dismal effects."

XXXVIII.

[Indorsed, " *With advice abt H. C. and how to arrange our separation and her Residence.*"]

DUBLIN. *Janr* 18, 1724–5.

Sʀ,—I answer yʳ two Letters with the first opportunity of the Post. I have already often told you my Opinion, and after much Reflection—what

I think it will be most prudent for you to do—I see nothing new in the case, but some displeasing Circumstances which you mention, and which I look upon as probable Consequences of that Scituation you are in—What I would do in such a Case I have told you more than once are : I would give that Person such an Allowance as was Suitable to my Ability, to live at a distance, where no Noise would be made. As to the Violences you apprehend you may be drawn to, I think nothing could be more unhappy for that would be vous mettre dans votre tort ; which a wise Man would certainly avoyd. I do not wonder that you should see a neglect of domestic Care when all Reconciliation is supposed impossible, every body is encouraged or discouraged by *Motives*, and the meanest Servant will not act his Part if he be convinced that it will be impossible ever to please his Master. I am sure I have been more than once very particular in my Opinion upon this Affair ; and have supposed any other Friend to be in the same case. There are many good Towns at a great distance from you, where People may board reasonably, and have the Advantage of a Church and a Neighbourhood—

But what Allowance you are content to give must depend upon what you are able. I think such a Thing may be continued without making much

Noise, and the Person may be a good while absent as upon Health or Visits, till the Thing grows out of Observation or Discourse. I entirely approve of y^r choice of a Tutor for your Son, and he will consult Cheapness as well as other Circumstances.

I have been out of Order about 5 months and am just getting out of a Cold when my Deafness was mending—Sending you Papers by the Post would be a great Expence, and Sometimes the Post master kept them. But if any Carrier plyed between you and us, they might be sent by Bundles. They say Cadogan is to lose some of his Employm^{nts}, and I am told, that next Pacquet will tell us of Severall Changes—I was t'other day well enough to see the Ld. L^t and the Town has a thousand foolish Storyes of what passed between us; which indeed was nothing but old Friendship without a word of Politicks.

Notes on XXXVIII.

Lord Cadogan had succeeded Marlborough as Commander-in-Chief. "As the great Duke reviewed us," writes Esmond, "riding along our lines with his fine suite of prancing aides-de-camp and generals, stopping here and there to thank an officer with those eager smiles and bows of which his Grace was always lavish, scarce a huzzah could be got for him, though Cadogan, with an oath, rode up and cried,

'D—— you, why don't you cheer?"' Horace
Walpole quotes a couplet of "an excellent satiric
epitaph on Lord Cadogan by Bishop Atterbury, who
was glad to kill the Duke of Marlborough with the
same stone :—

> "'Ungrateful to th' ungrateful man he grew by,
> A bad, bold, blustering, bloody, blundering booby.'"

Sir Robert Walpole, and his brother-in-law Lord
Townshend, had succeeded in removing Carteret
from the post of Secretary of State to that of Lord-
Lieutenant of Ireland, but had failed in ousting
Cadogan and some others of the party.

According to one of the "foolish Storyes," Swift,
at a full levee, pushed his way up to the Lord-
Lieutenant, and in a loud voice reproached him for
issuing a proclamation against the Drapier—" 'a
poor shop-keeper whose only crime is an honest
attempt to save his country from ruin. I suppose
you expect a statue of copper will be erected to you
for this service done to Wood.' The whole assembly
were struck mute. The titled slaves shrunk into
their own littleness in the presence of this man of
virtue. For some time a profound silence ensued,
when Lord Carteret made this fine reply in a line
of Virgil :—

> "'Res dura et regni novitas me talia cogunt moliri.'"

> ("My cruel fate
> And doubts attending an unsettled state
> Force me.")

XXXIX.

[Indorsed, "*A little before H. C. and I parted.*"]

S^R,—Your letter come this moment to my Hand and the Messenger waits and returns tomorrow. You describe yourself as in a very uneasy way as to Burr. I know it not but I believe it will be hard to find any Place without some Objections. To be permitted to live among Relations, will have a fair face, and be looked on as generous and good-natured, and therefore I think you should comply, neither do I apprehend any Consequences from the Person if the rest of the Family be discreet, and you say nothing against that—I think it would be well if you had some Companions in your House with whom to converse, or else the Spleen will get the Better, at least in long winter Evenings, when you cannot be among your workmen nor allways amuse y^r self with reading.

We have had no new thing of any Value since the second Letter from Nobody (as they call it) the Author of those two Letters is sd to be a Lord's eldest son—The Drapier's five Letters and those two, and five or six Copyes of Verses are all that I know of, and those I suppose you have had.

The Talk now returns fresh that the Ld. L^t will soon leave us, and y^e D [Duke] of Newcastle

KNIGHTLEY CHETWODE.
(From his portrait at Woodbrook.)

[*To face page* 166.

succeed, and that Horace Walpole will be Sec^{ry} of State.

I am &c.

Jan 30th 1724–5.

NOTES ON XXXIX.

Swift's advice to Chetwode was like that given nearly forty years later by Dr. Johnson to a friend who had put away his wife : " Your first care must be to procure to yourself such diversions as may preserve you from melancholy and depression of mind, which is a greater evil than a disobedient wife."

The talk that the Lord-Lieutenant was soon to leave was false. Five years later Swift published a humorous *Vindication of his Excellency from the Charge of favouring none but Tories, High Church- men, and Jacobites.* He admitted that his Lordship "with a singularity scarce to be justified carried away from the University of Oxford more Greek, Latin, and philosophy than properly became a person of his rank. . . . I cannot omit," he con- tinues, " another weak side in his excellency. For it is known, and can be proved upon him, that Greek and Latin books might be found every day in his dressing-room, if it were carefully searched. . . . This mistaken method of educating youth in the knowledge of ancient learning and language is too apt to spoil their politics and principles. It has been therefore a great felicity in these kingdoms that the heirs to titles and large estates have a weakness in their eyes, a tenderness in their constitutions ; are not able to bear the pain and indignity of whipping, and, as the mother rightly expresses it, could never take to their books." Swift concludes by the following account of the appointments to offices made during his Excellency's government :—

" Whig Account.

To persons promoted to bishopricks, or removed to more beneficial ones, computed per annum	...	...	...	£10,050	0	0
To civil employments ...	...	...	...	9,030	0	0
To military commands	...	...	...	8,436	0	0
				27,516	0	0

Tory Account.

To Tories	...	...	...	...	£111	0	0
	Balance ...	...	...	£27,405	0	0 "

The Duke of Newcastle had succeeded Carteret as Secretary of State. He was not displaced by Horace Walpole, who was sent as Ambassador to France. Carteret was a second time Secretary of State in 1741, and a third time (as Earl Granville) for a few days in 1746, when he was again succeeded by Newcastle. Smollett, in *Humphry Clinker*, makes one of his characters say at the Duke's levee: "Since Granville was turned out there has been no minister in this nation worth the meal that whitened his periwig."

Horace Walpole was brother of Sir Robert Walpole, and uncle of the famous letter-writer— "old Horace," as he was called later on. His nephew records how one day he left the House of Commons to fight a duel, and at once returned, "so little moved as to speak immediately upon the Cambrick Bill, which made Swinny say, 'That it was a sign he was not *ruffled.*'" Ruffles, then in fashion, were made of cambric.

XL.

[Indorsed, "*About James Stopford's promise to indemnify me for debts of H. C.'s contracting.*"]

DUBLIN. *Febr. 20th* 1724–5.

S\^r,—I extracted the Articles you sent me, and I sent them to M\^r Stopford, and this morning he shewed me a Letter he intends for you to night, which I think shews he is ready to do all in his Power. That of contracting Debts he will give Bonds for; the others you can not well expect more than his Word, and you have the Remedy

in your Power.   So I hope no Difficulty will
remain.   I am very glad you are putting of
your Land, and I hope you will contract things
into as narrow a Circle as can consist with your
Ease, since your Son and other Children will now
be an Addition to your annuall Charge.

As soon as it is heard that I have been with
Folks in Power, they get twenty Storyes about the
Town of what has passed, but very little Truth.
An English Paper in print related a Passage of
two Lines writ on a Card, and the Answer, of
which Story four parts in five is false—The
Answer was writ by Sir W. Fownes.   The real
Account is a Trifle, and not worth the Time to
relate.   Thus much for that Passage in y^r
Letter.

As to Company, I think you must endeavor to
cotton with the Neighboring Clergy and Squires.
The days are lengthening and you will have a long
Summer to prepare y^{r}self for Winter.   You should
pass a month now and then with some County
Friends, and play at whist for sixpence—I just
steal this Time to write that you may have my
Opinions at the same Time with Mr Stopford's
Letter.   I do think by all means he and you
should be as well together as the Situation of
Things will admit, for he has a most universal

good reputation. I think above any young man in the Kingdom.

I am yr most obt &c. J. S.

Notes on XL.

Chetwode, who was to make his wife an allowance, feared she might incur debts for which the law would hold him answerable. Her brother was willing to give him bonds for repayment.

The "two Lines writ on a Card" may be those which Swift is said to have scratched on the window of the waiting-room in the castle :—

> "My very good Lord, 'tis a very hard task,
> For a man to wait here who has nothing to ask."

Under which Lord Carteret wrote :—

> "My very good Dean, there are few who come here,
> But have something to ask or something to fear."

"Sir William Fownes," wrote Swift, "had indeed a very good natural understanding, nor wanted a talent for poetry ; but his education denied him learning, for he knew no other language except his own." There is an interesting letter of his to Swift which shows that in 1732 there was no madhouse in Ireland. He himself, when Lord Mayor of Dublin, had "had six strong cells made at the workhouse for the most outrageous." But so many were brought that the Corporation refused to admit any for the future. " I own to you," he continues; " I was for some time averse to our having a public Bedlam, apprehending we should be overloaded with numbers under the name of mad. Nay, I was apprehensive our case would soon be like that in England ; wives and husbands trying who could first get the other to Bedlam." He had come to the conclusion that a madhouse must be built, " but in a spot of ground free from the neighbourhood of houses, for the cries of the outrageous would reach a great way."

Swift used to keep a record of his gains and losses at cards. " Whist " he sometimes spelled " whish," as the following account shows :—

Won.

Nov 8th. Ombr.	Percevl Barry	...	...	...	5. 8.
" Ombr and whish.	Raymd Morgan ...		...		2. 4.

XLI.

May 27th 1725.

S^R,—The Place I am in is 8 miles from the Post so it may be some days before I have convenience of sending this. I have recovered my hearing for some time, at least recovered it so as not to be troublesome to those I converse with, but I shall never be famous for acuteness in that Sense, and

am in daily dread of Relapses ; against which I
prepare my mind as well as I can ; and I have too
good a Reason to do so ; For my eyes will not suffer
me to read small Prints ; nor anything by Candle-
light, and if I grow blind, as well as deaf, I must
needs become very grave, and wise, and insignificant.
The Weather has been so unfavourable, and continues so, that I have not been able to ride above
once ; and have been forced for Amusem' to set Irish
Fellows to work, and to oversee them—I live in a
Cabin and in a very wild Country ; yet there are
some Agreeablenesses in it, or at least I fancy so,
and am levelling Mountains and raising Stones, and
fencing against inconveniencyes of a scanty Lodging,
want of vittalls, and a thievish Race of People.

I detest the world because I am growing wholly
unfit for it, and could be onely happy by never
coming near Dublin, nor hearing from it, or anything
that passes in the Publick.

I am sorry your Enemyes are so restless to
torment you, and truly against the opinion of
Philosophers I think, next to Health a man's
Fortune is the tenderest Point ; for life is a Trifle ;
and Reputation is supply'd by Innocence, but the
Ruin of a man's Fortune makes him a Slave, which
is infinitely worse than loss of Life or Credit ; when
a man hath not deserved either ; and I repent

nothing so much, as my own want of worldly wisdom, in squandring all I had saved on a Cursed Wall; although I had your Example to warn me, since I had often ventured to railly you for your Buildings; which have hindred you from that Command of money; you might otherwise have had. I have been told that Lenders of money abound; not from the Riches of the Kingdom, but by the want of Trade—but whether Chattles be good security I can not tell. I dare say Mr Lightburn will be able to take up what he wants, upon the Security of Land, by the Judgm^t of the H. [House] of Lords; and I reckon he is almost a Lawyer, and would make a very good Solliciter. I can give you no Encouragement to go out of your way for a visit to this dismal Place; where we have hardly room to turn our selves, and where we send five miles round for a lean sheep. I never thought I could battle with so many Inconveniencyes, and make use of so many Irish Expedients, much less could I invite any Friend to share in them; and we are 8 miles from Kells, the nearest habitable Place—These is the State of Affairs here. But I should be glad to know you had taken some Method to lump your Debts. I could have wished Mr Stopford had let me know his Intentions of travelling with Graham; I know not the Conditions he goes on, and there is but one

THE DRAPIER'S TRIUMPH.

[To face page 175.

Reason why I should approve of such a Ramble ; I
know all young Travellers are eager to travell again.
But I doubt whether he consults his Preferment, or
whether he will be able to do any Good to, un
Enfant gaté, as Graham is.   Pray desire him to
write to me.   I had rather your Son might have
the Advantage of his Care, than of his Chambers.

I read no Prints.   I know not whether we have
a new King, or the old : much less any thing of
Barber.   I did not receive any Packet from you.

I am ever y^r &c.

The 6 months are over, so the Discoverer of the
Draper will not get the 300^{ll} as I am told.   I hope
the Parlm^t will do as they ought, in that matter,
which is the onely publick thing, I have in my mind.

I hope you like Dr Delany's country Place and
am glad to find you among such Acquaintances,
especially such a Person as he.

Notes on XLI.

Swift was staying in Dr. Sheridan's country
retreat at Quilca, "a bleak spot among the wildest
of the Cavan heaths," about fifty miles north-west of
Dublin.

One November ten years later he thus described
the life he was leading there to his cousin, Mrs.
Whiteway :—" Here are a thousand domestic con-
veniences wanting ; but one pair of tongs in the

whole house ; the turf so wet that a tolerable fire is a miracle ; the kitchen is a cabin a hundred yards off and a half ; the house back and fore door always left open, which in a storm, our constant companion, threatens the fall of the whole edifice ; Madam as cross as the devil, and as lazy as any of her sister sows, and as nasty. These are some of our blind sides. But we have a good room to eat in, and the wife and lodgers have another, where the doctor often sits and seems to eat, but comes to my eating room (which is his study), there finishes his meal, and has a share of a pint of wine ; the other pint is left till night." The Dean was working at *Gulliver's Travels.* " I have employed my time," he wrote to Pope, " (beside ditching) in finishing, correcting, amending, and transcribing my travels in four parts complete, newly augmented and intended for the press, when the world shall deserve them, or rather when a printer shall be found brave enough to venture his ears. I like the scheme of our meeting after distresses and dispersions, but the chief end I propose to myself in all my labours is to vex the world rather than divert it ; and if I could compass that design without hurting my own person or fortune I would be the most indefatigable writer you have ever seen, without reading."

His sight had been long failing. Twelve years earlier he had told how Vanessa

" Imaginary charms can find
In eyes with reading almost blind."

In some pretty lines to Stella on her birthday he said :—

> " For nature always in the right
> To your decay adapts my sight;
> And wrinkles undistinguished pass,
> For I'm ashamed to use a glass;
> And till I see them with these eyes,
> Whoever says you have them, lies."

On another birthday he wrote to her—

> " This day then let us not be told
> That you are sick and I grown old;
> Nor think on our approaching ills,
> And talk of spectacles and pills."

He would not let art remedy the failings of nature ; "for, having by some ridiculous resolution, or mad vow, determined never to wear spectacles, he could make little use of books in his latter years."

The work which he was overseeing was some improvements, at his own expense, on his friend's land, with which he hoped to surprise him. " He had a canal cut, and at the end of it, by transplanting some young trees, he had formed an arbour, which he called Stella's Bower. Besides he had surrounded some acres of land with a stone wall." Sheridan had heard of what was going on, and on his arrival took not the slightest notice of the changes. " ' Confound your stupidity ;' said Swift, in a rage ; 'why, you blockhead, don't you see the great improvements I have been making here ?' ' Improvements ! Mr. Dean,' " and then he went on to make nothing of them.

Sheridan, in his turn, during Swift's absence, had an island made in the middle of the lake by throwing in stones wrapped in large bundles of heath. On the top green sods were laid, and several well-grown osiers were planted. "'How the water of the lake is sunk in this short time,' cried out Swift, 'to discover that island of which there was no trace before!' 'Greatly sunk indeed,' observed the Doctor, 'if it covered the tops of those osiers. Swift then saw he had been fairly taken in, and acknowledged that his friend had got the better of him."

He described the people of Cavan as "a thievish Race of People." "Oppressed beggars," he says in one of his letters, "are always knaves; and I believe there hardly are any other among us." In another letter speaking of Tipperary, he writes: "Every male and female from the farmer inclusive to the day labourer, is infallibly a thief, and consequently a beggar, which in this island are terms convertible." Arthur Young, in his *Tour in Ireland*, mentions the following things stolen on Lord Longford's estate in Westmeath: "Hinges, chains, locks, keys, new wheels of a car, stones out of a wall, turnips by cartloads, two acres of wheat plucked off in a night. How far," he continues, "it is owing to the oppression of the laws, it is impossible to say. They are much worse treated than the poor in England." At Castle Caldwell, Fermanagh, "the people," he says, "are remarkably given to stealing, particularly grass, timber and turf; and they bring up their children to *hoking* potatoes, that is artfully raising them, taking out the best roots, and then replanting them." At Sligo " they thieve everything they can lay their hands on ; they will unshoe the horses in the field." At Johnstown, Tipperary, he writes : " The poor are by no means to be accused of a general spirit of thieving. It arises from holding them too much in contempt, or from the improper treatment of their superiors." At Louth, on the estate of a good landlord, Chief Baron Forster, " the people are remarkably honest. In working his improvements he has lived in a house without shutters, bolts, and bars, and with it half-full of *spalpeens* [mean fellows] and yet never lost the least trifle—nor has he met with any depredations among his fences or planta-tions."

Swift in this letter says that " next to Health a man's Fortune is the tenderest Point." Three years earlier he had written to Vanessa, " Re-member that riches are nine parts in ten of all that is good in life, and health is the tenth."

The " Cursed Wall " was the one which he had built at a cost of £600 round " Naboth's Vine-yard."

The judgment in the House of Lords was in the case of the Rev. Stafford Lightburne, against some of Swift's cousins. It reversed certain decrees of the Irish Exchequer Court, and affirmed others. It seems to have confirmed land to Lightburne. Swift wrote to him congratulating him on his success.

To Mr. Stopford, in a letter dated, "Wretched Dublin, in miserable Ireland, Nov. 26, 1725," he wrote, "Come home by Switzerland; whence travel blindfold till you get here, which is the only way to make Ireland tolerable." It is clear that he placed Switzerland on much the same level as Ireland. Stopford's pupil seems to have been robbed, for in the same letter Swift says: "Your other correspondents tell me that Mr. G., beside his clothes, lost £200 in money, which to me you slur over."

On January 10, 1721, Swift wrote: "Of the character and person of King George I am utterly ignorant, nor ever had once the curiosity to inquire into either, living at so great a distance as I do, and having long done with whatever can relate to public matters." On November 26, 1725, he wrote: "Here is a great rumour of the King's being dead, or dying at Hanover, which has not the least effect on any passion in me."

John Barber was a London printer, "for whom," wrote Swift, "I got two or three employments when I had credit with the Queen's ministers. He entered into the South Sea scheme, and grew prodigiously rich; but by pursuing too far he lost two-thirds of his gains. However, he bought a house with some acres near Richmond, and another in London, and kept £50,000, which enabled him to make a figure in the city." He was Lord Mayor in 1732–3. "There are," he wrote to Swift, "a dozen persons in my house called Lord Mayor's Officers, who wear black gowns, and give from eight to nine hundred pounds for their places. One-third of the purchase goes to the city; the other two-thirds are mine." After he had held office for nine months he wrote: "I have been thought to be a lucky man; but this year fortune has been my foe, for I have had no death happened in my year (a fiddler excepted) yet, nor have made £500 in all."

On the publication of the Drapier's Fourth Letter, dated October 23, 1724, a reward of £300 was offered for the discovery of the author within six months. Lord Carteret wrote to the Duke of Newcastle on October 31, that the Archbishop of Dublin told him "that the person who wrote the pamphlet had some thoughts of declaring himself to be the author of it, adding that he believed he might safely put himself upon his country, and stand his trial. If his boldness be so great I am fully determined to summon him before the Council; and though I should not be supported by them as I could wish, yet I shall think it my duty to order his being taken into custody, and to detain him, if I can by law, till his Majesty's pleasure should be further signified to me. For if his offer of bail be accepted, and he forthwith set at liberty, after so daring an insult upon his Majesty's government, it is to be apprehended that riots will ensue. I con-

sulted my Lord Chief Baron Hale, who thinks the
case, if it should happen, so extraordinary as to
become a matter of state, and require the utmost
rigour. 'Tis the general opinion here that Doctor
Swift is the author, and yet nobody thinks it can be
proved upon him; though many believe he will be
spirited up to own it." Harding, the printer of the
Drapier's Letters, was thrown into prison, where he
died. Few constitutions were strong enough to
endure for many weeks the miseries of the gaols
of those days.

The Primate Boulter wrote on October 12, 1725:
" Dr. Delany is one of the senior fellows of the
College here, and their greatest pupil-monger;
what with his fellowship and pupils he is thought to
have six or seven hundred pounds per annum." To
him Swift addressed some lines which begin :—

> " To you whose virtues I must own
> With shame, I have too lately known ;
> To you by art and nature taught
> To be the man I long have sought,
> Had not ill Fate, perverse and blind,
> Placed you in life too far behind ;
> Or, what I should repine at more,
> Placed me in life too far before ;
> To you the Muse this verse bestows.
> Which might as well have been in prose ;
> No thought, no fancy, no sublime,
> But simple topics told in rhyme."

In an interesting book Delany defended his
friend's memory against Lord Orrery's attacks.

His widow, who as Mrs. Pendarves had corresponded with Swift, was the "dear Mrs. Delany" of
Madame D'Arblay's Diary.   Miss Burney recorded
in 1786: " I went through Swift's letters to her,
Dr. Young's and Mr. Mason's, and destroyed all
that could not be saved every way to their honour."
Of her letters to the Dean there are ten in print,
but of his replies only three.[1]   " It is supposed,"
writes the editor of her Correspondence, " that the
rest were given *or taken* by friends, for autographs."
Some, perhaps, were thus lost; for the loss of others
Miss Burney's priggishness is answerable.   Mrs.
Pendarves described to her sister how in January,
1733, she met Swift at " the witty club " which
every Thursday dined at Dr. Delany's.   " In such
company," she wrote, " you may believe time
passed away very pleasantly.   Swift is a very *odd
companion* (if that expression is not too familiar for
so extraordinary a genius); he talks a great deal
and does not require many answers; he has infinite
spirits, and says abundance of good things in his
common way of discourse.   Miss Kelly's beauty
and good-humour have gained an entire conquest
over him, and I come in only *a little by the by*."
Dining there again in April she wrote: " The
Dean was there in *very good humour*, he calls him-

---

[1] There are only three included in *The Autobiography and
Correspondence of Mrs. Delany*. Mr. Elwin gives an extract
from a fourth, dated August 6, 1735. See his *Works of Pope*,
vii. 33, note.

self '*my master*,' and corrects me when I speak bad
English, or do not pronounce my words correctly."

Swift wrote to her on January 29, 1735-6:
" Dr. Delany hath long given up his house in town.
His Dublin friends seldom visit him till the swallows come in. He is too far from town for a winter
visit, and too near for staying a night in the country
manner; neither is his house large enough; it
minds me of what I have heard the late Duchess
[of Northumberland] complain, that Sion House
was 'a hobbedehoy, neither town nor country.'"

When of the "witty club" no one was left but
the aged Mrs. Delany, Delville was still not without
the charm of letters. It was the town house of
Bishop Percy, of Dromore, to whom we owe the
Reliques of Ancient English Poetry.

XLII.

July 19th 1725.

S^R,—I had y^rs of the 10th and y^r former of earlye
date. Can you imagine there is anything in this
Scene to furnish a Letter? I came here for no
other Purpose but to forget and to be forgotten. I
detest all News or Knowledge of how the World
passes. I am again with a Fitt of Deafness. The
Weather is so bad and continues so beyond any

Example in memory, that I cannot have the Beneffit of riding and I am forced to walk perpetually in a great Coat to preserve me from Cold and wett, while I amuse myself with employing and inspecting Laborers digging up and breaking Stones, building dry Walls, and cutting thro Bogs, and when I cannot stir out, reading some easy Trash merely to divert me.   But if the Weather does not mend, I doubt I shall change my Habitation to some more remote and comfortable Place, and there stay till ye Parlm^t is over, unless it sits very late.

I send this directed as the former, not knowing how to do better, but I wonder how you can continue in that Dirty Town.   I am told there is very little Fruit in the Kingdom, and that I have but 20 Apples where I expected 500—I hear Sale expected Harrison's whole Estate, and is much disappointed. Harrison's Life and Death were of a piece and are an Instance added to Millions how ridiculous a Creature is Man.

You agree with all my Friends in complaining I do not write to them, yet this goes so far that my averseness from it in this Place has made me neglect even to write on Affairs of great Consequence to my Self.   -

I am y^r most obd^t &c.

Notes on XLII.

"That Dirty Town" was probably Dublin. A
few months later Swift dated a letter : "Wretched
Dublin, in miserable Ireland," and ended it by
saying : "Pray God bless you, and send you safe
back to this place, which it is a shame for any man
of worth to call his home." Mrs. Pendarves wrote
of it in 1731 : "I must say the environs are
delightful. The town is bad enough, narrow
streets and dirty-looking houses, but some very
good ones scattered about."

On July 12 of this year Swift had written to a
friend : "We have had but five good days these
twelve weeks." A month later he wrote : "The
weather continues as foul as if there had not been
a day of rain in the summer, and it will have some
very ill effect on the Kingdom."

"How ridiculous a Creature is Man" Swift was
at this time doing his best to show in his *Gulliver's
Travels*. In this same year he described himself
as "sitting like a toad in a corner of his great
house, with a perfect hatred of all public actions
and persons." When the kindly Arbuthnot read
Gulliver's Travels he wrote to Swift : "Gulliver is
a happy man that at his age can write such a merry
work."

XLIII.

S^R,—You are to understand that I design to stay out a night, being no very active Rider, and it is very possible that may be inconvenient to you : I know not what to say nor how far your civility carryes you beyond your Ease. In that case I should be under much constraint. But if the journey be what you are inclined to, and that you think Mr Archdeacon Walls and me worth riding so far with, I will contrive to have y^r Mare reedy saddled for my selfe between six and seven to-morrow morning at the Deanery-House, which the Archdeacon tells me is directly in the way.

I am S^r your most obedient humble serv^t,

J: SWIFT.

Thursday 9 at night.

NOTES ON XLIII.

Though Swift calls himself "no very active Rider," nevertheless in his visits to England he used to go on horseback all the way between either Holyhead or Chester and London. In 1734 he wrote : " I ride every fine day a dozen miles on a large Strand or Turnpike road." Seven years before his death he wrote : " I seldom walk less than four miles, sometimes six, eight, ten or more, never beyond my own limits ; or, if it rains, I walk

as much through the house, up and down stairs ;
and if it were not for the cruel deafness I would
ride through the Kingdom, and half through
England."

We have now reached the last batch of Swift's
letters. The correspondence which opened so
briskly has grown sluggish with the lapse of time.
In the beginning of their acquaintance Swift wrote
more frequently to Chetwode in ten months than
we now find him writing in five or six years. For
a while his attention was drawn away from his
friends in Ireland by two visits which he paid to
England, and by the hopes raised in him by the
accession of a new king. His health, moreover,
was failing, and the attacks of giddiness and deafness from which he had suffered much in late years,
returned oftener and lasted longer. His thoughts
were narrowed, finding their centre in his own
misery. Nevertheless, he is still ready to help his
friend with his counsel for some time, till at last
neglect on his part, or perhaps only the suspicion
of neglect, leads to a quarrel. They close their
correspondence with bandying insults.

XLIV.

[Indorsed, "*Dr. Swift from London in answer to a Letter I wrote him concerning Cadenus and Vanessa.*" *Sent by hand.*]

LONDON. *Apr* 19*th* 1726.

S^R,—I have the Favor of y^r Lettr of the 7th instant. As to the Poem you mention, I know severall Copyes of it have been given about, and Ld. L^t [Lord-Lieutenant] told me he had one. It was written written [*sic*] at Windsor near 14 years ago, and dated: It was a Task performed on a Frolick among some Ladyes, and she it was addresst to dyed some time ago in Dublin, and on her Death the Copy shewn by her Executor. I am very indifferent what is done with it, for printing cannot make it more common than it is; and for my own Part, I forget what is in it, but believe it to be onely a cavalier Business, and they who will not give allowances may chuse, and if they intend it maliciously, they will be disappointed, for it was what I expected, long before I left Irel^d— Therefore what you advise me, about printing it my self is impossible, for I never saw it since I writ it, neither if I had, would I use shifts or Arts, let People think of me as they please. Neither do I believe the gravest Character is answerable for a

Private humersome thing which by an accident inevitable, and the Baseness of particular Malice is made publick. I have borne a great deal more, and those who will like me less, upon seeing me capable of having writ such a Trifle so many years ago, may think as they please, neither is it agreeable to me to be troubled with such Accounts, when there is no Remedy and onely gives me the ungratefull Task of reflecting on the Baseness of Mankind, which I knew sufficiently before.

I know not y^r Reasons for coming hither. Mine were onely to see some old Friends before my Death, and some other little Affairs, that related to my former Course of Life here. But I design to return by the End of Summer. I should be glad to be settled here, but the inconvenience and Charge of onely being a Passenger, is not so easy, as an indifferent home ; and the Stir people make with me, gives me neither Pride nor Pleasure. I have s^d enough and remain S^r y^{rs} &c.

NOTES ON XLIV.

Swift had left England on the Queen's death, and was now revisiting it for the first time after an absence of more than eleven years. " I was discouraged from going," he wrote, in 1724, " by considering what a scene I must expect to find by the death and exile of my friends, and a thousand other disgusting circumstances ; and after all, to return back again into this enslaved country to which I am condemned during existence—for I cannot call it life—would be a mortification hard to support." Pope, in a letter dated March 22, 1725–6, says : " Swift is in perfect health and spirits, the joy of all here who know him, as he was eleven years ago."

The poem, as we are told on the title-page, was " written at Windsor, 1713." The first five months of that year Swift spent in London. In June, July, and August he was in Ireland. On a pressing summons he had returned early in September. It was the eve of the election of a new parliament, and fierce was the fight between the Tories and Whigs over the Peace of Utrecht. Within the ministry the struggle had already begun between Lord Treasurer Oxford and Secretary Bolingbroke. Swift, moreover, had his own troubles about his tithes and rents. It seems almost impossible that at such a time *Cadenus and Vanessa* could have been written—a poem not only of great length, but, to use Goldsmith's description of it, " one of Swift's correctest pieces " and written " with elegant ease." In the autumn of that year the newly-made Dean spent perhaps three or four weeks at Windsor, with the interruption of at least one visit to London. If it was in 1713 that *Cadenus and Vanessa* was written, it was in these few and busy weeks. He tells Chetwode, however, that he wrote it near fourteen years before April, 1726. This would place the composition in the summer or autumn of 1712. Now in the late summer of that year he was a great deal at Windsor. Vanessa and her family, as one of her letters shows, were to join him there. The two lovers long preserved some memories connected with the town. Ten years later Swift wrote to her : " Go over the scenes of Windsor. . . . Cad thinks often of these." " Remember the indisposition at Windsor," he wrote in another letter about the same time. It is remarkable that this very same summer there is a great gap in his *Journal to Stella.* He who had scarcely let a day go by without writing now wrote only once between July 19th and September 15th. We would willingly believe that while he was describing how Vanessa and he " temper love and books together," he found it almost impossible to tell poor Stella in their "little language " how dear she was to him. A couplet in the poem seems to fix 1712 as the year of its composition. He tells how—

> " Vanessa, not in years a score,
>   Dreams of a gown of forty-four."

He was forty-four in the autumn of that year.

If my supposition is true the poem must have been revised and have received its title a year later, for it was not till the spring of 1713 that he was made a dean. There was no Decanus in 1712. In that case it might, with no great impropriety, have been described as written in 1713, that being the year in which it was completed.

Swift makes two statements about Vanessa which seem irreconcilable. On August 14, 1711, he wrote to Stella : " Mrs. Vanhomrigh's eldest daughter is come of age." On February 14 of the same year he mentioned that he had kept " Mrs. Vanhomrigh's daughter's birthday." If, as is asserted by the biographers, Vanessa was the elder of the two daughters, she was according to these statements born in 1690.[1] This is not consistent with the couplet which I have quoted above where he makes her nineteen when he was forty-four. As his birthday was November 30, 1667, she must in that case have been born at the end of 1692 or in 1693.

She died in May, 1723, " laying," it was said, " a strong injunction on her executors (Dr. Berkeley, afterwards Bishop Berkeley, and Robert Marshall, afterwards a judge in the Court of Common Pleas, Ireland) that immediately after her decease they should publish all the letters that had passed between Swift and her, together with the poem of *Cadenus and Vanessa.*" Of all this there is no mention in her will. The letters, we are told, were

[1] In her father's will, dated June 2, 1701, his children are mentioned in the following order—-Esther, Mary, Ginkell, and Bartholomew. This seems to show that she was the eldest of the children.

printed, but not published ; for Dr. Sheridan prevailed on the executors to cancel the copy.   Many
of them, however, "gradually found their way to the
public"; the entire correspondence was first given
in Scott's edition of Swift's Works.   I infer from
the Dean's letter to Chetwode that the poem was
not printed till 1726.   The "copyes given about"
were in manuscript.   The earliest edition in the
British Museum is of that year—" published and
sold by Allan Ramsay, at his shop at the East
end of the Lucken-booths [Edinburgh], price sixpence."   It is interesting to find the Scotch poet
thus connected with *Cadenus and Vanessa.*   The
" accident inevitable " by which it was made public
was, no doubt, Vanessa's death ; whose was " the
Baseness " can scarcely be doubted.   It was " by
her executor," Swift tells Chetwode, not by her
executors, that " the copy was shewn."   Berkeley
was the last man to work mischief against any
one.   Moreover, Swift had always been a friend
to him.   So late as September, 1724, when
Vanessa had been in her grave nearly a year and
a half, the Dean recommended him to the Lord-
Lieutenant as "one of the first men in this Kingdom
for learning and virtue."   Pope shared in this admiration.   He wrote to Swift in 1729 : " I am of
the religion of Erasmus, a Catholic ; so I live, so I
shall die ; and hope one day to meet you, Bishop
Atterbury and the younger Craggs, Dr. Garth,
Dean Berkeley, and Mr. Hutchinson in that place

to which God of his infinite mercy bring us and everybody." Some years later on the poet praised him in that well-known couplet where he says—

> "Manners with candour are to Benson given ;
> To Berkeley, every virtue under heaven."

Had Swift believed Berkeley guilty of "the baseness of particular malice," Pope would certainly have known it. It must have been Robert Marshall, the other executor, that he attacked.

Swift, it seems probable, soon got over the impossibility of printing the poem himself. At all events he was staying in Pope's house when, in a letter of the poet's to Benjamin Motte, the bookseller, dated June 30, 1727, mention is made of the reprinting of *Cadenus and Vanessa*.

The lines particularly dwelt on by those who "intended it maliciously" were the following :—

> "But what success Vanessa met
> Is to the world a secret yet.
> Whether the nymph to please her swain
> Talks in a high romantic strain ;
> Or whether he at last descends
> To act with less seraphic ends ;
> Or, to compound the business, whether
> They temper love and books together ;
> Must never to mankind be told,
> Nor shall the conscious Muse unfold."

The poet Tickell, who was Secretary to the Lords Justices of Ireland, had also written to Swift about the publication of the poem, who replied to him on July 7, 1726 : " The thing you mention, which no friend would publish, was written fourteen years ago at Windsor,[1] and shews how indiscreet it is to leave any one master of what cannot without the least consequence be shewn to the world. Folly, malice, negligence, and the incontinence in keeping secrets (for which we want a word) ought to caution men to keep the key of their cabinets."

The stir people made with Swift in London was foretold by Dr. Arbuthnot, who wrote to him, " I know of near half a year's dinners where you are already bespoke." Some years later the Dean describing this visit said : " Her present Majesty [Queen Caroline then Princess of Wales] heard of my arrival, and sent at least nine times to command my attendance before I would obey her. . . . At last I went, and she received me very graciously. I told her the first time : ' That I was informed she loved to see odd persons ; and that, having sent for a wild boy from Germany, she had a curiosity to see a wild dean from Ireland.'" On July 20, 1726, he wrote to Stopford : " I was latterly twice with the chief minister [Sir Robert Walpole] the first time by invitation, and the second at my desire for an hour, wherein we differed in every point." The Primate, Boulter, on February 10, 1725, had written to Walpole, who put great trust in him : " The general report is that Dean Swift designs for

[1] Sir Walter Scott is wrong in saying : " This must have been the Windsor Prophecy."

England in a little time ; and we do not question his endeavours to misrepresent his Majesty's friends here, wherever he finds an opportunity ; but he is so well known, as well as the disturbances he has been the fomentor of in this Kingdom, that we are under no fear of his being able to disserve any of his Majesty's faithful servants by anything that is known to come from him." It was in vain that Swift represented to Walpole "that the whole country of Ireland, except the Scottish plantation in the north, is a scene of misery and desolation hardly to be matched on this side Lapland," and that the grievances under which the English inhabitants suffered " had been all brought upon that Kingdom since the Revolution." " I failed very much in my design," he wrote.

It can scarcely be doubted, that he had hoped to effect an exchange of preferments so that he might return to England, but in this he was disappointed. Had he been more yielding he might perhaps have succeeded. After his departure for Ireland, Pope wrote to him : " I had a conference with Sir Robert Walpole, who expressed his desire of having seen you again before you left us ; he said he observed a willingness in you to live among us, which I did not deny." Swift in his *History of the Four Last Years of Queen Anne* speaks of his enemy as "one Mr. Robert Walpole." So too we find in various writers: "one William Wallace"; "one Mr. Milton, a blind man "; " one Prior "; " one Gay, a

poet"; "one Handel, a foreigner"; "one Johnson"; "one Boswell"; "one Robert Burns," and
"one Montaigne."

Besides the hope of settling in England Swift
had another object in his visit. He had to find "a
printer bold enough to venture his ears" in the
publication of *Gulliver's Travels*.

XLV.

DUBLIN. *Octr 24th* 1726.

S^R,—Since I came to Ireland to the time that I
guess you went out of Town, I was as you observe
much in the Country, partly to enure my self gradually to the Air of this place and partly to see a Lady
of my old Acquaintance who was extremely ill. I
am now going on the old way having much to do of
little consequence, and taking all advantages of fair
weather to keep my Health by walking. I look
upon you as no very warm Planter who could be
eighteen months absent from it, and amusing y^r self
in so wretched a Town as this, neither can I think
any man prudent who hath planting or building going
on in his absence.

I believe our discoursing of Friends in Engl^d would
be very short, for I hardly imagine you and I can
have three of the same Acquaintance there, Death

JONATHAN SWIFT.
(By Markham, after Bindon.)

[*To face page* 198.

and Exil having so diminished the number ; and as for Occurences, I had as little to do with them as possible, my Opinions pleasing very few ; and therefore the life I led there was most in the Country, and seeing onely those who were content to visit me, and receive my Visits, without regard to Party or Politicks. One thing I have onely confirmed my self in, which I knew long ago, that it is a very idle thing for any man to go for England without great Business, unless he were in a way to pass his Life there, which was not my Case, and if it be yours, I shall think you happy.

I am as always an utter Stranger to Persons and occurences here — and therefore can entertain you with neith[r], but wish you Success in this season of planting, and remain

Yr most faithfull &c.

Notes on XLV.

Swift left London on August 17. He wrote to a friend : " I suppose I shall be in Dublin, with moderate fortune, in ten or eleven days hence; for I will go by Holyhead." He travelled faster than he expected, for in a letter to Pope [1] he speaks of " the quick change I made in seven days from London to the Deanery, through many nations and languages

[1] This letter, as Mr. Craik points out, though, as published, it is dated October 30, 1727, refers to Swift's return in 1726.

unknown to the civilised world.   And I have often
reflected in how few hours with a swift horse or a
strong gale a man may come among a people as
unknown to him as the antipodes."   At Dublin " he
was brought to the landing-place in a kind of
triumph.   The boats were adorned with streamers,
and he was conducted to his house by a multitude of
his grateful countrymen, amid repeated acclamations
Long live the Drapier.'   The bells were all set
a-ringing and bonfires kindled in every street."

" Lady Carteret, wife of the Lord-Lieutenant,
said to Swift, ' The air of this country is good.'   He
fell down on his knees.   ' For God's sake, madam,
don't say so in England ; they will certainly tax it.' "

The " Lady of my old acquaintance who was
extremely ill " was Stella.   On July 15 he had
written to a friend in Dublin from Pope's house :
" What you tell me of Mrs. Johnson I have long
expected with great oppression and heaviness of
heart.   We have been perfect friends these thirty-
five years.   Upon my advice they both [she and
Mrs. Dingley] came to Ireland, and have been ever
since my constant companions ; and the remainder
of my life will be a very melancholy scene when
one of them is gone, whom I most esteemed
upon the score of every good quality that can
possibly recommend a human creature. . . . Let
her know I have bought her a repeating gold watch
for her ease in winter nights.   I designed to have
surprised her with it ; but now I would have her

know it, that she may see how my thoughts are
always to make her easy." In another letter he
writes : " There hath been the most intimate friendship between us from our [1] childhood, and the
greatest merit on her side that ever was in one
human creature towards another. . . . I have been
long weary of the world, and shall for my small
remainder of years be weary of life, having for
ever lost that conversation which could only make it
tolerable." He was troubled by the fear that she
might die in the Deanery, which she was occupy-
ing in his absence. "You know it cannot but be
a very improper thing for that house to breathe
her last in." She lived a year and a half longer,
dying on January 28, 1728.

He wished much to be settled in England.
During his visit there he wrote to a friend : "This
is the first time I was ever weary of England, and
longed to be in Ireland ; but it is because go I
must ; for I do not love Ireland better, nor England,
as England, worse ; in short you all live in a
wretched, dirty doghole and prison, but it is a place
good enough to die in." Three years later he
wrote from Dublin : "You think, as I ought to
think, that it is time for me to have done with the
world ; and so I would, if I could get into a better,

---

[1] Perhaps Swift wrote ,"from her childhood," as he was nearly
fourteen years the elder. When he first saw her he was a young
man.

before I was called into the best, and not die here in
a rage, like a poisoned rat in a hole."

XLVI.

DUBLIN. *Feb* 14*th* 1726–7.

S^R,—I should have sooner answered y^r Lett,.
[your Letter] if my time had not been taken up with
many impertinences, in Spight of my Monkish way
of living ; and particularly of late—with my preparing a hundred little affairs which must be
dispatched before I go for England, as I intend to
do in a very short time, and I believe it will be the
the last Journey I shall ever take thither.   But the
omission of some Matters last summer, by the absence
of certain people hath made it necessary.   As to
Captn Gulliver, I find his book is very much censured
in this Kingdom which abounds in excellent Judges ;
but in Engl^d I hear it hath made a bookseller almost
rich enough to be an Alderman.   In my Judgment
I should think it hath been mangled in the press,
for in some parts it doth not seem of a piece, but I
shall hear more when I am in England.   I am glad
you are got into a new Tast of your Improvements,
and I know no thing I should more desire than some
Spot upon which I could spend the rest of my life

in improving.   But I shall live and dye friendless,
and a sorry Dublin inhabitant ; and yet I have
Spirit still left to keep a clutter about my little
garden, where I pretend to have the finest paradise
Stockes of their age in Ireland.   But I grow so old,
that I despond, and think nothing worth my Care
except ease and indolence, and walking to keep my
Health.

I can send you no news, because I never read
any, nor suffer any person to inform me.   I am sure
whatever it is it cannot please me.   The Archb^r
of Dublin is just recovered after having been
despaired of, and by that means hath disappointed
some hopers.

I am S^r y^r &c.

NOTES ON XLVI.

Swift more than once mentions his " Monkish way
of living."   In one letter he speaks of the years " all
monastically passed in this country of liberty, and
delight, and money, and good company."   In another
letter he writes : " I am as mere a monk as any in
Spain ; I eat my morsel alone like a king, and am
constantly at home when I am not riding or walking,
which I do often and always alone."

On November 8, 1726, Arbuthnot had written to
him from London : " *Gulliver's Travels*, I believe,
will have as great a run as John Bunyan.   It is in

everybody's hands.   Lord Scarborough, who is no
inventor of stories, told me that he fell in company
with a master of a ship, who told him that he was
very well acquainted with Gulliver; but that the
printer had mistaken ; that he lived in Wapping, and
not in Rotherhithe.   I lent the book to an old gentleman who went immediately to his map to search
for Lilliput."   Gay wrote a few days later : " The
whole impression sold in a week.   From the highest
to the lowest it is universally read, from the cabinet
council to the nursery."   " Here is a book come
out," wrote Lady Mary Wortley Montagu, " that all
our people of taste run mad about : 'tis no less than
the united work of a dignified clergyman, an eminent
physician, and the first poet of the age [Swift,
Arbuthnot and Pope]."

Swift used to leave the profits of his writings to
the booksellers.   In 1735 he wrote : " I never got a
farthing by anything I writ, except one about eight
years ago, and that was by Mr Pope's prudent
management for me."   The time of publication
renders it almost certain that this one book was
Gulliver's Travels.   He is said to have received
£300.   His cousin, Mrs. Whiteway, wrote to Pope
in 1740 : " *The History of the Last Four Years of
Queen Anne's Reign*, if I am rightly informed, is the
only piece of his, excepting *Gulliver*, which he ever
proposed making money by."   It was not, however,
published till some years after his death.   For
editing the third part of Sir William Temple's

Memoirs he had received £40; how much he was paid for the earlier parts is not known. By the Irish edition of *Gulliver*, published in 1727, he made nothing. "Dublin booksellers," he said, "have not the least notion of paying for a copy [copyright]." To a London bookseller he wrote: "You send what books you please hither, and the booksellers here can send nothing to you that is written here. As this is absolute oppression, if I were a bookseller in this town I would use all the safe means to reprint London books, and run them to any town in England that I could, because whoever offends not the laws of God, or the Country he lives in, commits no sin." The Irish booksellers needed no encouragement in this respect. They bribed one of Richardson's printers to steal for them the sheets of *Sir Charles Grandison*, while it was going through the press.

That "Gulliver was mangled in the press" vexed Swift greatly. On November 17, 1726, keeping up the mystery of authorship, he wrote to Pope: "I read the book over, and in the second volume observed several passages which appear to be patched and altered, and the style of a different sort, unless I am mistaken." On January 3rd of the following year, Charles Ford, who was staying in Dublin, wrote to Motte blaming him for the gross errors of the press in which the book abounded and sending him a few corrections. This letter has been preserved and is in the John Forster Library in the

South Kensington Museum.   It is clear that though
the whole is in Ford's handwriting, it was composed
by Swift.   It was in the fifth and sixth chapters of
the *Voyage to the Houyhnhnms* that the text had
been most mangled.   The printer, from fear of his
ears,   had   weakened   the   satire   on   lawyers   and
ministers of state.   In Ford's letter are such passages as the following : " Vol. ii. p. 69 &c., mani-
festly most barbarously corrupted, full of Flatnesses,
Cant Words, and Softenings unworthy the Dignity,
Spirit, Candour and Frankness of the Author.   By
that admirable Instance of the Cow it is plain the
Satyr is design'd against the Profession in general,
and   not   only   against   Attorneys,   or,   as   they   are
there   smartly   styl'd   Pettifoggers.   You   ought   in
Justice to restore those twelve Pages to the true
Reading."

" Part of 90 and 91 false and silly infallibly not
the same Author.   I take this Page to be likewise
corrupted from some low Expressions in it."

The printer, in spite of Ford's reproaches, which
he must have known really came from Swift, did not
venture on more than verbal corrections.

More   than   six   years   later,   on   June   29,   1733,
Swift   wrote   to   Ford : " Now   you   may   please   to
remember   how   much   I   complained   of   Motte's
suffering some friend of his (I suppose it was Mr.
Took, a clergyman, now dead) not onely to blot
out some things that he thought might give offense,
but to insert a good deal contrary to the author's

manner and style and intention. I think you had a Gulliver interleaved and set right in those mangled and murdered pages. I enquired of several persons where that copy was. Some said Mr. Pilkington had it, but his wife sent me word that she could not find it. . . . To say the truth, I cannot with patience endure that mingled and mangled manner as it came from Motte's hands, and it will be extremely difficult for me to correct it by any other means, with so ill a memory and so bad a state of health." Six weeks later he wrote to the same friend : " Motte tells me he designs to print a new edition of Gulliver in quarto, with cuts and all as it was in the genuine copy. He is very uneasy about the Irish edition. All I can do is to strike out the trash in the edition to be printed here. It was to avoid offence that Motte got those alterations and insertions to be made. I suppose by Mr. Took, the clergyman deceased, so that I fear the second edition will not mend the matter further than as to literall faults. For instance, the Title of one Chapter is of the Queen's Administration, without a Prime Minister, and accordingly in the chapter it is said that she had no chief Minister &c. Besides the whole sting is absent out of several passages in order to soften them. Thus the style is debased, the humour quite lost, and the matter insipid."

This interleaved *Gulliver* is also in the John

Forster Library. The text as corrected in it was first printed in the Dublin edition of 1735.[1]

To this edition Swift prefixed the *Letter from Captain Gulliver to his Cousin Sympson written in the Year 1727.* It is likely enough that the letter really was written at that time in the expectation that Motte would make use of it. At all events it is clear that the author wished his readers to know that he was now giving them the text as it originally stood. In this letter he says : " I do not remember I gave you power to consent that anything should be omitted, and much less that anything should be inserted : Therefore, as to the latter, I do here renounce everything of that kind, particularly a paragraph about her majesty Queen Anne, of most pious and glorious memory, although I did reverence and esteem her more than any of the human species. But you, or your interpolator, ought to have considered that, as it was not my inclination, so was it not decent to praise any animal of our composition before my master Houyhnhnm ; and besides the fact was altogether false ; for to my knowledge, being in England during some part of her majesty's reign, she did govern by a chief minister; nay, even by two successively ; the first whereof was the Lord of Godolphin, and the

---

[1] An addition to the *Voyage to Laputa* was apparently overlooked. It was first printed in Mr. George A. Aitken's appendix to the edition of *Gulliver's Travels* published in 1896 by Messrs. J. M. Dent & Co.

second the Lord of Oxford, so that you have made me say the thing that was not."

Ford, in his letter to Motte, speaking of the same paragraph, had said: "It is plainly false in Fact, since all the World knows that the Queen during her whole Reign governed by one first Minister or other. Neither do I find the Author to be anywhere given to Flattery or indeed very favourable to any Prince or Minister whatsoever." The Rev. Mr. Took had flattered the Queen in the title of Chapter VI. of Part IV., which had originally stood: "A Continuation of the State of England; The Character of a first or chief Minister of State in European Courts." In the first edition this had been changed into: "A Continuation of the State of England; so well governed by a Queen as to need no first Minister. The Character of such an one in some European Courts." In the Chapter itself a page and a half had been inserted which Swift directed the printer to blot out. Motte had not even dared to print the famous passage correctly where Swift laughs at the orders of the Garter, Bath and Thistle. The three fine silken threads with which the Emperor of Lilliput rewarded the agility of his courtiers, instead of being blue, red and green, were in the first edition purple, yellow and white.

This was the second time that the Archbishop of Dublin by his recovery "disappointed some hopers." Three years earlier than the date of the letter in the text, the Primate Boulter had written to the Duke of Newcastle : " The Archbishop of Dublin has of late been very ill. I think his Majesty's service absolutely requires that whenever he drops the place be filled with an Englishman." He recovered enough from this second attack to vex Swift, who, writing to him on May 18th of this year about "the visitation of the Dean and Chapter," said : " I see very well how personal all this proceeding is ; and how, from the very moment of the Queen's death, your Grace has thought fit to take every opportunity of giving me all sorts of uneasiness, without ever giving me, in my whole life, one single mark of your favour beyond common civilities. . . . Neither my age, health, humour or fortune qualify me for little brangles ; but I will hold to the practice delivered down by my predecessors." To Dr. Sheridan he wrote on June 24th about the same matter : " I will spend a hundred or two pounds rather than be enslaved, or betray a right which I do not value threepence, but my successors may."

XLVII.

DUBLIN. *Novr* 23*rd* 1727.

S^R,—I have yours of the 15th instant, wherein you tell me that upon my last leaving Ireland, you supposed I would return no more, which was probable enough, for I was nine weeks very ill in

England, both of Giddyness and Deafness, which latter being an unconversable disorder I thought it better to come to a place of my own, than be troublesome to my Friends, or live in a lodging; and this hastened me over, and by a hard Journy I recovered both my Aylments. But if you imagined me to have any favor at Court you were much mistaken or misinformed. It is quite otherwise at least among the Ministry. Neither did I ever go to Court, except when I was sent for and not always then. Besides my illness gave me too good an excuse the last two months.

As to Politicks; in Engl^d it is hard to keep out of them, and here it is a shame to be in them, unless by way of Laught^r [Laughter] and ridicule, for both which my tast is gone. I suppose there will be as much mischief as Interest, folly, ambition and Faction can bring about, but let those who are younger than I look to the consequences. The publick is an old tattred House but may last as long as my lease in it, and therefore like a true Irish tenant I shall consider no further.

I wish I had some Retirement two or three miles from this Town, to amuse my self, as you do, with planting much, but not as you do, for I would build very little. But I cannot thing of a remote Journey

in such a miserable country, such a Clymat, and
such roads, and such uncertainty of Health. I
would never if possible be above an hour distant
from home—nor be caught by a Deafness and
Giddyness out of my own precincts, where I can do
or not do, what I please ; and see or not see, whom
I please. But if I had a home a hundred miles off
I never would see this Town again, which I believe
is the most disagreeable Place in Europe, at least
to any but those who have been accustomed to it
from their youth, and in such a Case I suppose a
Jayl might be tolerable. But my best comfort is,
that I lead here the life of a monk, as I have
always done; I am vexed whenever I hear a
knocking at the door, especially the Raps of quality,
and I see none but those who come on foot. This
is too much at once.

I am y^r &c.

Notes on XLVII.

Swift had paid a second visit to England early
in April. It ended unhappily and he never came
again. His old ailments returned in great force.
He had lived too well at Pope's house ; and so he
thought had brought back his giddiness. "Cyder
and champaign and fruit," he wrote, "have been
the cause." His deafness was worse than ever. "I

have," he said, "a hundred oceans rolling in my
ears, into which no sense has been poured this
fortnight." He described the state of himself and
his friend in the following verses :—

"Pope has the talent well to speak,
　But not to reach the ear ;
His loudest voice is low and weak,
　The Dean too deaf to hear.

A while they on each other look,
　Then different studies choose ;
The Dean sits plodding on a book ;
　Pope walks, and courts the Muse."

On his return to Dublin he wrote to the poet :
"I have thought it best to return to what fortune
has made my home. . . . Here is my maintenance
and here my convenience. If it pleases God to
restore me to my health I shall readily make a third
journey; if not, we must part as all human creatures
have parted. . . . Two sick friends never did well
together; such an office [the care of a sick friend]
is fitter for servants and humble companions, to
whom it is wholly indifferent whether we give them
trouble or not. . . . I have a race of orderly,
elderly people of both sexes at command, who
are of no consequence, and have gifts proper for
attending us ; who can bawl when I am deaf, and
tread softly when I am only giddy and would sleep."
He was alarmed moreover by bad news of Stella.
Writing to Sheridan about a letter just received

from him he said : " I kept it an hour in my pocket
with all the suspense of a man who expected to
hear the worst news that fortune could give him,
and at the same time was not able to hold up his
head. These are the perquisites of living long ;
the last act of life is always a tragedy at best ; but
it is a bitter aggravation to have one's best friend
go before one. . . . What have I do in the world ?
I never was in such agonies as when I received
your letter, and had it in my pocket."

To add to his misery his hope of a settlement in
England was lost for ever. In May he had written
to this same friend : " It is certain that Walpole is
peevish and disconcerted, stoops to the vilest offices
of hireling scoundrels to write Billingsgate of the
lowest and most prostitute kind, and has none but
beasts and blockheads for his penmen whom he
pays in ready guineas very liberally. I am in high
displeasure with him and his partisans." George I.
was known to be failing in health, and Swift, like
many another, looked forward with some hope to
the new reign. " I have," he wrote, " at last seen
the princess, twice this week by her own commands;
she retains her old civility and I my old freedom ;
she charges me without ceremony to be the author
of a bad book [*Gulliver's Travels*], though I
told her how angry the ministry were ; but she
assures me that both she and the prince were very
well pleased with every particular." He counted
also on the favour of Mrs. Howard, the Prince's

mistress. He was on the point of starting for France when the news came from Hanover of the King's death. "Since then," he wrote, "we have been all in a hurry with millions of schemes. I deferred kissing the King's and Queen's hands till the third day, when my friends at Court chid me for deferring it so long. . . . I was with great vehemence dissuaded from going to France by certain persons whom I could not disobey." Mrs. Howard was one of those who dissuaded him, and Bolingbroke was another. "Much less," his Lordship wrote to him, "ought you to think of such an unmeaning journey, when the opportunity for quitting Ireland for England is, I believe, fairly before you."

Swift thought that Walpole's power was at end. "It is agreed," he wrote, "the ministry will be changed, but the others will have a soft fall; although the King must be excessive generous if he forgives the treatment of some people." Walpole, no doubt, is aimed at here. The very day on which this was written the great minister was restored to power. "There I am sure I see a friend," said the Queen at her first drawing-room, looking at his wife, who was almost hidden behind a great crowd. Instantly the whole company made way. She approached the Queen and kissed her hand. She told her son that "in returning she might have walked upon their heads, so eager were they to pay their court to her." Swift's last chance had gone. He had laid his stake on the wrong horse.

His " hard Journy" was the long ride from London to Holyhead, in Wales, where he was kept some days by contrary winds, "in a scurvy unprovided comfortless place without one companion," as he wrote in his Journal. " I cannot read at night, and I have no books to read in the day. I am afraid of joining with passengers for fear of getting acquaintance with Irish. The days are short, and I have five hours at night to spend by myself before I go to bed. I should be glad to converse with farmers or shopkeepers, but none of them speak English. A dog is better company than the vicar, for I remember him of old. The Master of the pacquet boat, one Jones, hath not treated me with the least civility, altho' Watt gave him my name. In short I come from being used like an Emperor to be used worse than a Dog at Holyhead. Yet my hat is worn to pieces by answering the civilities of the poor inhabitants as they pass by. Pray pity poor Wat, for he is called dunce, puppy, and liar 500 times an hour, and yet he means not ill, for he means nothing. Oh ! for a dozen bottles of deanery wine and a slice of bread and butter. If the vicar could but play at back-gammon I were an Emperor ; but I know him not. I am as insignificant here as Parson Brooke is at Dublin. By my conscience, I believe Cæsar would be the same without his army."

His taste for ridicule of Irish politicians was not wholly gone. A few years later he attacked them in the lines beginning—

> " Ye paltry underlings of state ;
> Ye senators, who love to prate ;
> Ye rascals of inferior note,
> Who for a dinner sell a vote ;
> Ye pack of pensionary peers,
> Whose fingers itch for poets' ears ;
> Ye bishops far removed from saints,
> Why all this rage ? why these complaints ? "

The life he led in Dublin he thus described to Pope : " I keep humble company, who are happy to come when they can get a bottle of wine without paying for it. I give my vicar a supper and his wife a shilling to play with me an hour at backgammon once a fortnight. To all people of quality and especially of titles I am not within ; or at least am deaf a week or two after I am well."

Even when he was a much younger man he did not take a cheerful view of " the publick." So early as 1709, in a letter to Archbishop King, he says : " The world is divided into two sects, those that hope the best, and those that fear the worst ; your Grace is of the former, which is the wiser, the nobler, and most pious principle ; and although I endeavour to avoid being of the other, yet upon this article I have sometimes strange weaknesses."

Mrs. Pendarves, in 1732, after crossing the island from Dublin to Killala, wrote : " The roads are

much better in Ireland than England, mostly cause-
ways, a little jumbling, but *very safe*." In 1742,
after she had visited Down Patrick, she wrote: "I
never travelled such fine roads as are all over this
country." In the winter of 1750, writing of returning home by moonlight from a friend's house, she
said: "A comfortable circumstance belonging to
this country is, that the roads are so good and free
from robbers that we may drive safely any hour of
the night."

Arthur Young, who visited Ireland in 1776, thus
writes of the roads: "A turnpike in Ireland is a
synonymous term for a vile road; the bye roads are
the finest in the world. It is the effects of jobs and
imposition which disgrace the Kingdom."

Though Mrs. Pendarves had not been "accustomed to Dublin from her youth," and though she
was by birth a Granville, nevertheless, by no means
did she find that town " the most disagreeable Place
in Europe." On her first visit to Ireland in 1731
she wrote: "There is a heartiness among the
people that is more like Cornwall than any I have
known, and great sociableness." On her return to
England in 1733 she wrote to her sister: "I wish
you and I could be conveniently transported to
Ireland for one year; no place could suit your taste
so well; the good-humour and conversableness of
the people would please you extremely."

XLVIII.

DUBLIN. *Decbr* 12*th* 1727.

S^R,—I thought to have seen your Son, or to have spoken to his Tutor. But I am in a condition to see nobody ; my old disorder of Deafness being returned upon me, so that I am forced to keep at home and see no company ; and this disorder seldom leaves me under two months.

I do not understand your son's fancy of leaving the University to study Law under a Teacher. I doubt he is weary of his Studyes, and wants to be in a new Scene ; I heard of a fellow some years ago who followed that practice of reading Law, but I believe it was to Lads, who had never been at a University ; I am ignorant of these Scheams, and you must advise with some who are acquainted with them. I only know the old road of getting some good learning in a university and when young men are well grounded then going to the Inns of Court. This is all I can say in the matter, my Head being too much confused by my present Disorder.

I am y^r obd^t &c.

NOTES ON XLVIII.

Swift in his Letter to a Young Clergyman says : " What a violent run there is among too many weak people against university education : be firmly assured that the whole cry is made up by those who were either never sent to a college, or, through their irregularities and stupidity, never made the least improvement while they were there." The students of Dublin University he thus mentions in a letter to Pope : "You are as much known here as in England, and the university lads will crowd to kiss the hem of your garments."

Wherever young Chetwode studied law, he would have had to learn law Latin. For four years longer it was to remain the language of the records in the law courts. Blackstone in his Commentaries sighs over the change that was made, when, by act of Parliament, English alone was to be thenceforth used. The common people, he said, were as ignorant in matters of law as before, while clerks and attorneys were now found who could not understand the old records. Owing, moreover, to the verbosity of English, more words were used in legal documents, to the great increase of the cost.

XLIX.

DUBLIN. *Mar.* 15*th* 1728-9.

S^R,—I had the favor of yours of the 5th instant, when I had not been above a fortnight recovered from a disorder of giddyness and Deafness, which hardly leaves me a month together. Since my last return from Engl^d I never had but one Letter from you while I was in the Country, and that was during a time of the same vexatious ailment, when I could neither give my self the trouble to write or to read. I shall think very unwise in such a world as this, to leave planting of trees, and making walks, to come into it—I wish my fortune had thrown me any where rather than into this Town and no Town, where I have not three acquaintances, nor know any Person whom I care to visit. But I must now take up with a solitary life from necessity as well as Inclination, for yesterday I relapsed again, and am now so deaf that I shall not be able to dine with my Chapter on our onely festival in the year, I mean St. Patrick's Day. As to any Scurrilityes published against me, I have no other Remedy, than to desire never to hear of them and then the authors will be disappointed, at least it will be the same thing to me as if they had never been writ. For I will not imagine that any friend I esteem, can value me the less, upon the Malice of Fools, and knaves, against whose Republick I have always been at open War. Every man is safe from Evil tongues, who can be content to be obscure, and men must take Distinction as they do Land, cum onere.

I wish you happy in your Retreat, and hope you will enjoy it long and am your &c.

Notes on XLIX.

Swift had passed eight months of 1728-9 at Market Hill, Armagh, the seat of .Sir Arthur Acheson. On August 2, 1728, he wrote from that place to Dr. Sheridan : " I am well here, and hate removals. . . . My reason for staying is to be here the planting and pruning time, &c. I hate Dublin, and love the retirement here, and the civility of my hosts." On February 13, 1729, after his return home, he wrote to Pope : " I lived very easily in the country ; Sir Arthur is a man of sense and a scholar, has a good voice, and my lady a better ; she is perfectly well bred and desirous to improve her understanding, which is good, but cultivated too much like a fine lady. She was my pupil there, and severely chid when she read wrong ; with that, and walking, and making twenty little amusing improvements, and writing family verses of mirth by way of libels on my lady, my time passed very well, and in very great order ; infinitely better than here, where I see no creature but my servants and my old Presbyterian housekeeper, denying myself to everybody till I shall recover my ears." In another letter he says : " I had at least half a dozen returns of my giddiness and deafness, which lasted me about three weeks a-piece. . . . When this disorder is on me I have neither spirits to write, or read, or think, or eat." It was at Market Hill that he wrote one of his most lively pieces—*Hamilton's Bawn.*

In W. M. Mason's *History of St. Patrick's Cathedral* (page 291) there is given the following bill of the festival on St. Patrick's Day, 1715, " endorsed by Swift, in his own hand-writing, ' The chapter dinner, 17 March, 1715 ' "—

	£	s.	d.
For Coals		3	o
For Lemons, Chessnuts, Oringes, and Wall-nutts ...		5	o
For Sallmon...		6	o
For Codd, Whitings, Flounders and other fish... ...		5	5½
For Lobsters		10	10
Calfes head		2	6
Meate for Gravy			6
Calfes feete and Palletes			10
A side of Lamb		4	6
For Butter		9	4
For Teals, Partridgs, Growes and Quails		16	10
For Bread		3	o
For Creame			8
For Charcoale		1	6
Sallett, by his bill		7	11
Oyesters		3	4
Surloyne of Beefe		6	10
Flower		1	6
Musturd			2
Cleane Man			6
Eggs			6
Chees			6
	4	11	5½
Wine from Clackston		14	o
Nellson the Cook bill	1	10	o
May's bill for Wine	1	5	10
Alle and Beere		6	2
Wine by Nellson		3	o
Cook Wages		6	o
Washinge ye Linen		1	6
	8	17	11½

In July, 1732, Swift wrote : "I have in twenty years drawn above one thousand scurrilous libels on myself, without any other recompense than the love of the Irish vulgar, and two or three dozen signposts of the Drapier in this city, besides those that are scattered in country towns ; and even these are half worn out."

His war against the republic of fools and knaves he thus speaks of in his *Lines on the Death of Dr. Swift* :—

> "As with a moral view designed
> To cure the vices of mankind,
> His vein ironically grave
> Exposed the fool and lashed the knave."

The reverse of the safety from evil tongues that is found in obscurity he has thus expressed : "Censure is the tax a man pays to the public for being eminent."

L.

Dublin. *May* 17*th* 1729.

S^R,—That I did not answer your former Letter, was because I did not know it required any, and being seldom in a tolerable humor by the frequent returns or dreads of Deafness, I am grown a very bad correspondent. As to the passage you mentioned in that former Letter, and desired my opinion, I did not understand the meaning, and

that Lett[r] being mislayd, I cannot recollect it, tho'
you refer to it in your last. I shall not make the
usuall excuses on the subject of lending money, but
as I have not been master of 30[ll] for thirty days
this thirty years, so I have actually borrowed
severall small Sums for thesse two or three years
past for board-wages to my Serv[ts] [Servants] and
common expences. I have within these ten days
borrowd the very poor money lodged in my
hands, to buy Cloaths for my Servants, and left
my note in the bag in case of my Death. These
pinches are not peculiar to me, but to all men in
this Kingdom, who live upon Tythes or rack [?]
rents, for, as we have been on the high road to ruin
these dozen years, so we have now got almost to
our Journey's End: And truly I do expect and am
determined in a short time to pawn my little plate,
or sell it, for subsistance. I have had the same
request you make me, from severall others, and
have desired the same favor from others, without
Success; and I believe there are hardly three men
of any figure in Irel[d], whose affairs are so bad as
mine, who now pay Interest for a thous[d] pounds of
other peoples money (which I undertook to manage)
without receiving one farthing my self, but engaged
seven years in a law suit to recover it. This is the
fairest side of my Circumstances for they are worse

than I care to think of, much less to tell, and if the
universall complaints and despair of all people have
not reacht you, you have yet a vexation to come.
I am in ten times a worse state than you, having a
lawsuit on which my whole fortune depends, and
put to shifts for money which I thought would
never fall to my lot.   I have been lately amazed as
well [as] grieved at some intimate friends, who
have desired to borrow money of me, and whom
I could not oblige but rather expected the same
kindness from them.

Such is the condition of the Kingdom, and such
is mine.

I am y^r &c.

Notes on L.

Swift in his letters often complains of the want
of ready money.   " Money," he once wrote, " is
not to be had, except they will make me a bishop,
or a judge, or a colonel, or a commissioner of the
revenues."   Nevertheless, on his death, ten years
after this was written, he left more than £11,000.
It is not true that he had " not been master of 30^{ll}"
for thirty days this thirty years."   In 1712 he had
£400 in the hands of a friend; in 1725 he lost
£1,250 by another friend's ruin.   This very year
Gay wrote to him about £200 which he had in
Lord Bathurst's hands, who wished to repay it.   In

the miserable poverty of the farmers, however, he found great difficulty in collecting his tythes and rents. On August 11th he wrote to Pope: "As to this country there have been three terrible years' dearth of corn, and every place strewed with beggars; but dearths are common in better climates, and our evils here lie much deeper. Imagine a nation, the two-thirds of whose revenues are spent out of it, and who are not permitted to trade with the other third." He described in the sixth number of *The Intelligencer* a ride he took of sixty miles through the best part of the Kingdom. Everywhere wretchedness met his view. "In short," he concludes, "I saw not one single house in the best town I travelled through which had not manifest appearances of beggary and want."

A few years later he wrote to Arbuthnot: "My Revenues by the miserable oppressions of this Kingdom are sunk to 300ll a year; I live at two thirds cheaper here than I could there [in London]. . . . I can buy a Chicken for a Groat, and entertain three or four friends with so many dishes and two or three Bottles of French Wine for 11 shill. When I dine alone my Pint and Chicken with the Appendixes cost me about 15 pence." A little later still he wrote to Charles Ford: "I can hitherto dine on a morsel without running in debt, and I have been forced to borrow near 200*l.* to supply my small family of three servants and a half for want of any reasonable payments." The miserable state of the country is shown by the following quotations from the Primate Boulter's letters to the English ministers :—

"Feb. 24, 1727. When I went my visitation last year we met all the roads full of whole families that had left their homes to beg abroad, since their neighbours had nothing to relieve them with. This summer must be more fatal to us than the last, when I fear many hundreds perished by famine."

"July 16, 1728. I know some in Dublin who have occasion to pay workmen every Saturday night that are obliged to pay fourpence for every twenty shillings in silver they procure."

"May 2, 1730. Our manufactures and retail trade are under the last distress for want of silver."

"April 21, 1731. The ordinary people here are under the last distress for want of copper money. Tradesmen that retail and poor people are forced to pay for getting their little silver changed into copper, and are forced to take raps or counterfeit half-pence, of little more than a quarter of the value of an English halfpenny, which has encouraged several such coiners."

"May 25, 1736. We are almost on the brink of ruin by the present unhappy state of our money."

Wood's halfpence would have been far better than the scarcity and the "raps." At last Boulter was able to move the government to supply a remedy, as the two following entries show :—

" March 26, 1737. Two tons of our copper halfpence are arrived. Dean Swift has raised some ferment about them here, but people of sense are very well satisfied of the want and goodness of them."

" May 16, 1737. Notwithstanding all the clamours of Dean Swift, the papists, and other discontented or whimsical people, our new copper halfpence circulate and indeed are most greedily received."

Mrs. Pendarves wrote in June, 1732 : " The poverty of the people, as I have passed through the country, has made my heart ache ; I never saw greater appearance of misery ; they live in great extremes, either profusely or wretchedly." Nine months earlier, at a ball given at the Castle, she had found at supper everything prepared with great magnificence. " I never saw," she adds, " so much meat with so little confusion." In 1752 she wrote : " High living is too much the fashion here. You are not invited to dinner to any gentleman of a £1,000 a year or less that does not give you seven dishes at one course, and Burgundy and Champagne ; and these dinners they give once or twice a week that provision is now as dear as in London."

Swift always kept his servants on board wages " at the highest rate then known, which was four shillings a week." Their staying long in his service showed that with all his roughness he was not a bad master. There was one circumstance which gratified their pride. "The Dean's plain livery," we are told, "was a badge of greater distinction than that of the Lord-Lieutenant with all its finery." "He was served in plate, and used to say that he was the poorest gentleman in Ireland that ate upon plate, and the richest that lived without a coach."

His lawsuit, whatever it was, went on troubling him. Two years later he wrote to Gay : " I thought I had done with the lawsuit, and so did all my lawyers ; but my adversary, after being in appearance a Protestant these twenty years, has declared he was always a Papist, and consequently by the law here cannot buy, nor, I think, sell ; so that I am at sea again for almost all I am worth."

LI.

Aug. 9th 1729.

S^r ,—Your Lett^r of July 30th I did not receive till this day. I am near 60 miles from Dublin, and have been so these 10 weeks. I am heartily sorry for the two ocassions of the Difficultyes you are under. I knew Mrs Chetwode from her Child-hood, and knew her mother and Sisters, and although I saw her but few times in my life, being in a different Kingdom, I had an old friendship for her, without entring into differences between you, and cannot but regret her death. As to Mr Jackman I have known him many years, he was a good

MRS. CHETWODE
(From her portrait at Woodbrook.)

[To face page 230.

natured generous and gentlemanly person ; and a
long time ago, having a little money of my own,
and being likewise concerned for a friend, I was
inclined to trust him with the management of both
but received some hints that his affairs were even
then not in a condition so as to make it safe to
have any dealings of that kind with him. For
these 14 years past, he was always looked upon as
a gone man, for which I was sorry, because I had
a personal inclination towards himself, but seldom
saw him of late years ; because I was onely a
generall acquaintance, and not of intimacy enough
to advise him, or meddle with his affairs, nor able
to assist him. I therefore withdrew, rather than
put my Shoulders to a falling wall, which I had no
call to do. This day upon reading y^r Lett^r I asked
a Gentleman just come from Dublin, who told me
the Report was true, of Jackman's being gone off.
Now S^r I desire to know, how it is possible I can
give you Advice being no Lawyer, not knowing
how much you stand engaged for, nor the Situation
of your own Affairs. I presume the other Security
is a responsible person, and I hope Mr Jackman's
arrears cannot be so much as to endanger your
sinking under them. It is to be supposed that M^r
Shirley will give time, considering the case. I
think there is a fatality in some people to embroyl

themselves by their good nature. I know what I would do in the like condition ; It would be, upon being pressed, to be as open as possible, and to offer all in my power to give Satisfaction, provided I could have the allowance of time. I know all fair Creditors love free and open dealings, and that staving off by the arts of Lawyers makes all things worse at the end. I will write to Mr Stopford by the next post, in as pressing a manner as I can ; he is as honest and benevolent a person as ever I knew. If it be necessary for you to retrench in your way of living, I should advise, upon supposing that you can put your affairs in some Settlement here under the control of your Son assisted by some other friends, that you should retire to some town in England in a good country and far from London, where you may live as cheap as you please, and not uncomfortably, till this present Storm shall blow over. This is all I can think of after three times reading your Letter. I pray God direct you ;

I am ever &c.

Note on LI.

Two days after the date of this letter Swift wrote to Pope : " My head is never perfectly free from giddiness, and especially toward night. Yet my disorder is very moderate, and I have been without a fit of deafness this half year ; so I am like a horse which, though off his mettle, can trot on tolerably ; and this comparison puts me in mind to add that I am returned to be a rider. . . . Was it a gasconade to please me that you said your fortune was increased £100 a year since I left you? Those *subsidia senectuti* are extremely desirable if they could be got with justice and without avarice ; of which vice, though I cannot charge myself yet, nor feel any approaches toward it, yet no usurer more wishes to be richer, or rather to be surer of his rents."

LII.

Aug. 30th 1729.

S^{R},—I received your Lett^{r} by a man that came from Dublin with some things for me. This is the first post since ; I come now to answer y^{r} questions. First whether you shall marry. I answer that if it may be done with advantage to your fortune, to a person where the friendship and good usage will be reciprocall, and without loss to y^{r} present children, I suppose all y^{r} friends, as I, would approve it. As to the affair of Lettr of Licence &c. I profess I am not master of it. I understand it is to be given by all the Creditors before the Debtor can be secure; why it is desired of you, I know not, unless as a Creditor.

and how you are a Creditor, unless as being bound for him, I am as ignorant, and how Jackman in his condition can be able to indemnify you is as hard to conceive; I doubt his rich friends will hardly do it. This is all I can see after half blinding my self with reading yr Clerks Copyes. As to y^r leaving Irel^d, doubtless y^r first step should be to London for a final answer from the Lady ; if that fayls, I think you can live more conveniently in some distant southern county of Engl^d, tho' perhaps cheap^r in France. To make a conveyance of y^r estate etc. there must I suppose be advice of good Lawyers. Mr Stopford will be a very proper person, but you judge ill in thinking on me who am so old and crazy, that for severall years I have refused so much as to be Executor to three or four of my best and nearest friends both here and in Engl^d. I know not whether Mr Stopford received my Letter: but I will write to him again. You cannot well blame him for some tenderness to so near a Relation, but I think you are a little too nice and punctilious for a man of this world, and expect more from human race, than their Corruptions can afford. I apprehend that whatever the debt you are engaged for shall amount to, any unsettled part of your estate will be lyable to it, and it will be wise to reckon upon no assistance from Jackman, and if you shall be forced to raise money and pay Interest, you must look onely towards how much is left, and either retrieve by marriage or live retired in a thrifty way.   No man can advise otherwise than as he follows himself.   Every farthing of any temporall fortune I have is upon the balance to be lost.   The turn I take is to look on what is left, and my Wisdom can reach no higher.   But as you ill bear publick Mortifications it will be best to retire to some oth^r Country where none will insult you on account of your living in an humbler manner.   In the Country of England one may live with repute, and keep the best company for 100^l a year.   I can think of no more at present.   I shall soon leave this place, the weather being cold, and an Irish winter country is what I cannot support.

I am S^r y^r most &c.

Notes on LII.

Swift's assertion that "no man can advise otherwise than as he follows himself" would have brought on him the reproach from Johnson that he was "grossly ignorant of human nature."   When it was objected that a certain medical author did not practice what he taught, Johnson replied: "That does not make his book the worse.   People are influenced more by what a man says, if his practice is suitable to it, because they are blockheads."

That a man living by himself could, in those days, on £100 a year keep the best company in the country parts of England is confirmed by a curious statement published by Boswell of Peregrine Langton, who in a Lincolnshire village, on £200 a year had done much more than this, for he had kept up a house with four servants, a post-chaise and three horses.

Arthur Young states that at Bury St. Edmunds in 1741, as his mother's memorandum book shows, beef and veal were three pence a pound, and mutton three pence halfpenny. Fielding, in *Joseph Andrews*, says that Parson Adams "at the age of fifty was provided with a handsome income of twenty-three pounds a year; which, however, he could not make any great figure with, because he lived in a dear country, and was a little encumbered with a wife and six children."

LIII.

DUBLIN. *Feby 12th* 17$\frac{29}{30}$.

S^{R},—I did not come to town till October, and I solemnly protest that I writ to you since I came, with the opinion I was able to give on the affairs you consulted me about; indeed I grow every day an ill retainer of memory even in my own affairs, and consequently much more of other peoples, especially where I can be of little or no Service.

I find you are a great Intelligencer, and charge me
at a venture with twenty things which never came
into my head.   It is true I have amused my self
sometimes both formerly and of late, and have
suffered from it by indiscretion of people.   But I
believe that matter is at an end ; For I would see
all the little rascals of Ireland hanged rather than
give them any pleasure at the expence of disgusting
one judicious friend.—I have seen Mr Jackman
twice in the Green and therefore suppose there
hath been some expedient found for an interval of
liberty : but I cannot learn the state of his affairs.
As to changing your Single life, it is impossible to
advise without knowing all circumstances both of
you and the Person.   A. B^p Sheldon advised a
young Lord to be sure to get money with a wife
because he would then be at least possessed of
one good thing.   For the rest, you are the onely
judge of Person, temper and understanding.   And,
those who have been marryed may form juster
ideas of that estate than I can pretend to do.

I am S^r your most obd^t &c.

NOTES ON LIII.

Of a lord who, acting up to Archbishop Sheldon's
advice, had married for money, Johnson said :
" Now has that fellow at length obtained a

certainty of three meals a day, and for that
certainty, like his brother dog in the fable, he
will get his neck galled for life with a collar."

The Archbishop's advice, if we can trust the
report given of him, was not always so worldly.
" His advice to young noblemen and gentlemen,
who by the order of their parents daily resorted to
him, deserves to be mentioned. It was always
this : ' Let it be your principal care to become
honest men, and afterwards be as devout and
religious as you will. No piety will be of any
advantage to yourselves or anybody else unless
you are honest and moral men.' " A bad report,
however, reached Pepys of his Grace's character.
On July 29, 1667, he records : " My cosen
Roger told us as a thing certain, that the Archbishop of Canterbury that now is do keep a wench,
and that he is as very a wencher as can be . . .
which is one of the most astonishing things that I
have heard of." Burnet says of Sheldon : " He
had a great pleasantness in conversation perhaps
too great. . . . He seemed not to have a deep
sense of religion, if any at all." He does not,
however, accuse him of looseness of life. The
Archbishop's name is kept alive in the Sheldonian
Theatre at Oxford, which he founded.

Swift in the last lines of his letter implies that he
had never been married. Writing nine years later
to Alderman Barber he speaks of himself and his
correspondent as " we two old bachelors." So like-

STELLA'S COTTAGE.

[To face page 231.

wise Esther Johnson in her will describes herself as "spinster." That he had been married there is evidence which satisfied Dr. Johnson and Sir Walter Scott, as it had satisfied Swift's second cousin, Deane Swift; who was twenty years old at the time of Stella's death. The proofs against the marriage were first marshalled by W. Monck Mason in his *History of St. Patrick's Cathedral*, published in 1819. Of his later biographers Mr. Forster "can find no evidence of it that is at all reasonably sufficient." Mr. Churton Collins utterly disbelieves in it; in this view he is supported by Mr. Stanley Lane-Poole who maintains that "the 'evidence' has been laughed out of court." Mr. Leslie Stephen writes: "On the whole, though the evidence has weight, it can hardly be regarded as conclusive. Sir Henry Craik agrees with Johnson and Scott. An argument against marriage may be drawn —perhaps has already been drawn—from the three prayers which Swift used for her in her last sickness. In these, evidently written with deep feeling and a strong sense of religion, he would scarcely have kept hidden, as it were, from his God, that he and the poor sufferer were husband and wife.

Of marriage Swift wrote in his *Thoughts on Religion:* "No wise man ever married from the dictates of reason."

LIV.

DUBLIN. *June 24th* 1730.

S^r,—I had yours but it came a little later than usuall; you are misinformed; I have neither amused my self with opposing or defending any body. I live wholly within my self; most people have dropt me, and I have nothing to do, but fence against the evils of age and sickness as much as I can, by riding and walking; neither have I been above 6 miles out of this town this 9 months; except once at the Bish^{ns} [Bishop's] visitation in Trim. Neither have I any thought of a Villa eith^r near or far off; having neither money, youth, nor inclination for such an atchievement. I do not think the Country of Ireland a habitable scene without long preparation, and great expense. I am glad your trees thrive so well. It is usuall when good care is taken, that they will at last settle to the ground.

I cannot imagine how you procure enemyes, since one great use of retirement is to lose them, or else a man is no thorow retirer. If I mistake you not, by your 60 friends, you mean enemies; I knew not Webb.—As to your information of passages in private life, it is a thing I never did nor shall pursue; nor can envy you or any man for knoledge in it; because it must be lyable to great mistakes, and consequently wrong Judgments. This I say, though

I love the world as little, and think as ill of it as
most people ; and I would as lieve peep three hours
a morning into a jakes. Mr Cusack dyed a week
after I left Trim ; and is much lamented by all
Partyes. What embroylments you had with him I
know not ; but I always saw him act the part of a
generous, honest, good natured, reasonable, obliging
man. I find you intended to treat of a marriage by
Proxy in Engl^d and the lady is dead. I think you
have as ill luck with burying your friends, as good
with burying your enemyes ; I did expect that
would be the event when I heard of it first from you.
I know not what advertisements you read of any
Libels or Storyes against me, for I read no news ;
nor any man tells me of such things, which is the
onely way of disappointing such obscure Slaunderers.
About 3 years ago I was shewn an advertisem^t to
some such purpose, but I thought the Person who
told me had better let it alone. I do not know
but they will write Memoirs of my actions in War ;
These are naturall consequences that fall upon people
who have writings layd to their charge, whether true
or not—

I am just going out of town, to stay no where
long, but go from house to house, whether Inns or
friends, for five or six weeks mearly for exercise.

I am S^r your most obedient &c.

I direct to Maryborow by guess, never remembering whether that or Mountmelick be right.

NOTES ON LIV.

A year later Swift wrote to Gay : " Valetudinarians must live where they can command and scold ; I must have horses to ride ; I must go to bed and rise when I please, and live where all mortals are subservient to me. I must talk nonsense when I please, and all who are present must commend it. I must ride thrice a week, and walk three or four miles besides every day." In a letter to Charles Ford, dated December 9, 1732, he says : " I do not think life is of much value, but health is worth everything, and nature acts right in making that method which prolongs life absolutely necessary to preserve health, which makes a short life and a merry a very foolish proverb. For my own part I labor daily for health as often and almost as many hours as ever man does for daily bread."

On December 24, 1736, he wrote to Lord Castle Durrow : " I dine almost constantly at home, because, literally speaking, I know not above one Family in this whole Town where I can go for a Dinner. The old Hospitality is quite extinguished by Poverty and the oppressions of England. . . . As to puddings, my Lord, I am not only the best, but the sole perfect maker of them in this Kingdom ; they are universally known and esteemed under the name of the

Deanry Puddings; Suit and Plumbs are three-fourths of the Ingredients; I had them from my Aunt Giffard, who preserved the succession from the time of Sir William Temple." Mrs. Pendarves these same years found a good deal of "the old hospitality." Thus of the Bishop of Killala's Dublin house she wrote: "A universal cheerfulness reigns in it. They keep a very handsome table, six dishes of meat are constantly at dinner and six plates at supper." Of a Mr. and Mrs. Hamilton she said: "Their house, like themselves, looks cheerful and neat. We had a very pretty supper neatly served." "At Mrs. Usher's," she added, "we are always handsomely entertained."

Though Swift says that he had "no thought of a Villa," nevertheless about this time, we are told, he had intended to build a house on some land which he took of Sir Arthur Acheson. It was to bear the name of Drapier's Hill. He celebrated it in the following lines :—

"We give the world to understand,
  Our thriving Dean has purchased land :
  A purchase which will bring him clear
  Above his rent four pounds a year ;
  Provided to improve the ground
  He will but add two hundred pound ;
  And from his endless hoarded store,
  To build a house, five hundred more
  Sir Arthur too shall have his will,
  And call the mansion Drapier's Hill ,
  That when a nation long enslaved
  Forgets by whom it once was saved ;

When none the Drapier's praise shall sing,
His signs aloft no longer swing,
His medals and his prints forgotten,
And all his handkerchiefs are rotten,[1]
His famous Letters made waste paper,
This hill may keep the name of Drapier;
In spite of envy flourish still,
And Drapier's vie with Cooper's Hill."

LV.

[*Knightley Chetwode to Dean Swift.*]

[No date.]

S^r,—I came to Towne ye 12th of Decr and leave
it the 12th of March, and could never see you but
in ye streete, the last time I met you I merryly
thought of Horace's 9th Satire, and upon it pursued
you to y^r next house tho' not "prope Cæsaris
hortos."—I had a desire to catch you by y^r best
ear for halfe an hour and something to tell you,
w^h I imagined w^d surprize and please you, but
with the cunning of experienced Courtiers, grown
old in politicks, you put me off with a I'll send
to you; w^h probably you never intended.   I am
now returning to Wodebrook from an amour w^h
has proved little profitable to myselfe—Business
here I 've none but with women; those pleasures
have not (with me) as yet [? lost] their charms

---

[1] "Medals were cast, many signs hung up, and handkerchiefs made with
devices in honour of the Dean, under the name of M. B. Drapier."

and tho' when I am at home I do not like my
neighbourhood and shall therefore probably seldom
stir beyond the limits of my gardens and Plantations, wh. are full big enough for my purse, or
what is even more insatiable my ambition, yet if
my amusements there are scanty my thoughts are
unmolested. I see not ye prosperity of Rascalls,
I hear not ye Complaints of the worthy—I enjoy
the sun and fresh air without paying a fruitless
attendance upon his Eminence of St. Patricks,
my fruit will bloom, my Herbs be fragrant, my
flowers smile tho' the Deane frowns, and looks
gloomy, take this as some sort of returne for y^e
greatest neglect of me, I 've mett since my last
coming to this Towne, many ill offices, and what
is far more extraordinary wth halfe a dozen Females
who have cleared up the truth of it to a mathe-
maticall demonstration; this causes me to reflect
upon the Jewishe method formerly to make Prose-
lytes w^h I think St. Ambrose well expresses in y^e
following words "Hi arte immiscent se hominibus,
Domos penetrant, ingrediuntur Prætoria, aures judi-
cum et publica inquietant, et ideo magis prævalent
quo magis impudenter." I saw you pass last friday
by my windowe like a Lady to take horse, with
y^r handcirchiefe and whipp in y^r hand together;
y^r petticoats were of ye shortest, and you wanted

a black capp or I might have thought of Lady Harriett Harley now Lady Oxford.

Notes on LV.

Lady Henrietta Cavendish Holles, heiress of Holles, Duke of Newcastle, had married Lord Harley, son of the Earl of Oxford, in 1713. Swift celebrated the marriage in verse. Bolingbroke described it, in a letter to the Dean, as "the ultimate end of a certain administration." The administration was the one in which he himself had held the post of Secretary of State. He asserted, and asserted it moreover to a man who had been deep in the confidence of the minister, that his chief, Lord Treasurer Oxford, in all his measures had had one end in view—to secure for his son the wealthiest heiress in England. Of this same Lord Treasurer Swift wrote : " I do impartially think him the most virtuous minister, and the most able that ever I remember to have read of." Both Bolingbroke and Swift wrote the history of their own time. Who can wonder that Sir Robert Walpole exclaimed : " Anything but history, for history must be false."

The second Lady Oxford had her troubles. Mrs. Pendarves wrote in 1741, just before the Earl's death : " My Lord Oxford has of late been so entirely given up to drinking that his life has been no pleasure to him or satisfaction to his

friends; my Lady Oxford never leaves his bed-
side, and is in great trouble.   He has had no
enjoyment of the world since his mismanagement
of his affairs."   It was with a folio belonging to
his library that Johnson beat Osborne, the bookseller.

LVI.

[Knightley Chetwode to Dean Swift.]

S^r,—I am truly concerned at y^r having been so
long lame which you say I can't see you, tho' I
imputed it to your having taken something amiss
in my last letter, wherein when I thought I was
only plaine perhaps I've been blunt, and y^t is a
fault for I am of opinion with my old friend
Wycherly, that some degree of ceremony sh^d
[should] be preserved in the strictest friendship.
However I write again to you, upon my old
maxim y^t [that] he who forbears to write because
his last letter is unanswered shews more regard
to forms and punctillios than to friendship. I 've
mett you handed about in print and as the Coffey
Houses will have it of your owne doing—I am
afraid y^r using y^r legg too soon will not let it be
too soon well, the very shaking of a chair tho'
yo had a stole under it, I believe harm'd you for

you see by y^r accident at ye A'p's visitation how small a thing throws you back. Beware I pray you of this hurt in time, for if a swelling sh^d fix in y^r leggs an access of a Dropsy may be apprehended—I sh^d be glad to see you if it were conven^t [convenient] and agreeable to you and not else, tho' I am y^r well wisher and humble Servt

K. C.

LVII.

[Dean Swift to Knightley Chetwode.]
[Indorsed, "*A very extraordinary lettr designed I suppose to mortifie me—within this letter are coppies of some lettrs of mine to him.*"]

DUBLIN. *May 8th* 1731 [? 1732].

S^r,—Your letter hath layen by me without acknowledging it, much longer than I intended, or rather this is my third time of writing to you, but the two former I burned in an hour after I had finished them, because they contained some passages which I apprehended one of your pique might possibly dislike, for I have heard you approve of one principle in your nature, that no man had ever offended you, against whom you did not find some opportunity to make him regret it, although perhaps no offence were ever designed. This perhaps, and

the other art you are pleased with, of knowing the
secrets of familyes, which as you have told me was
so wonderfull that some people thought you dealt
with old Nick, hath made many families so cautious
of you.   And to say the truth, your whole scheme of
thinking, conversing, and living, differ [*sic*] in every
point from mine.   I have utterly done with all great
names and titles of Princes and Lords and Ladyes
and Ministers of State, because I conceive they do
me not the least honor; wherein I look upon
myself to be a prouder man than you, who expect
that the people here should think more honorably
of you by putting them in mind of your high
acquaintance, whereas the Spirits of our Irish
folks are so low and little, and malicious, that they
seldom believe a syllable of what we say on these
occasions, but score it all up to vanity; as I have
known by Experience, whenever by great chance I
blabbed out some great name beyond one or two
intimate friends.   For which reason I thank God
that I am not acquainted with one person of title in
this whole Kingdom, nor could I tell how to behave
myself before persons of such sublime quality—
Half a dozen midling Clergymen, and one or two
midling laymen make up the whole circle of my
acquaintance—That you returned from an amour
without profit, I do not wonder, nor that it was

more pleasurable, if the Lady as I am told be sixty, unless her literal and metaphorical talents were very great ; yet I think it impossible for any woman of her age, who is both wise and rich, to think of matrimony in earnest. However I easily believe what you say that women have not yet lost all their charms with you—who could find them in a Sybel. I am sorry for what you say that your ambition is unsatiated, because I think there are few men alive so little circumstanced to gratify it. You made one little essay in a desperate Cause much to the disadvantage of your fortune, and which would have done you little good if it had succeeded ; and I think you have no merit with the present folks, though some affect to believe it to your disadvantage.

I cannot allow you my disciple ; for you never followed any one rule I gave you—I confess the Qu's [Queen's] death cured all ambition in me, for which I am heartily glad, because I think it little consists either with ease or with conscience.

I cannot imagine what any people can propose by attempts against you, who are a private country Gentleman, who can never expect any Employment or power. I am wondering how you came acquainted with Horace or St. Ambrose, since neither Latin nor Divinity have been your Studyes ; it

seems a miracle to me. I agree with that Gentleman (whoever he is) that said to answer letters was
a part of good breeding, but he would agree with
me, that nothing requires more caution, from the ill
uses that have been often made of them, especially
of letters without common business. They are a
standing witness against a man, which is confirmed
by a Latin saying—For words pass but Letters
remain. You hint I think that you intend for
England. I shall not enquire into your motives,
my correspondence there is but with a few old
friends, and of these but one who is in Employm^t,
and he hath lately dropt me too, and he is in right;
for it is said I am out of favor; at least, what I
like as well, I am forgotten, for I know not any one
who thinks it worth the pains to be my enemy; and
it is meer charity in those who still continue my
friends, of which however not one is in Power, nor
will ever be—during my life—I am ashamed of this
long letter, and desire your Pardon.

I am, S^r y^r &c.

Notes on LVII.

One of the suppressed letters written by Swift
to Chetwode at this time, he most certainly did
not burn. It was preserved, and was included
in his collected correspondence, though his editors

did not know for whom it was meant. It is as follows :—

To Ventoso.

April 28, 1731

Sir,—Your letter has lain by me without acknowledging it longer than I intended; not for want of civility, but because I was wholly at a loss what to say; for as your scheme of thinking, conversing and living differs in every point diametrically from mine, so I think myself the most improper person in the world to converse or correspond with you. You would be glad to be thought a proud man, and yet there is not a grain of pride in you; for you are pleased that people should know you have been acquainted with persons of great names and titles, whereby you confess that you take it for an honour; which a proud man never does: and besides you run the hazard of not being believed. You went abroad, and strove to engage yourself in a desperate cause, very much to the damage of your fortune, and might have been to the danger of your life, if there had not been, as it were, a combination of some who would not give credit to the account you gave of your transactions; and of others who, either really, or pretending to believe you, have given you out as a dangerous person; of which last notion I once hinted something to you; because, if what you repeated of yourself were true, it was necessary that you had either made your peace, or must have been prosecuted for high treason.

The reputation (if there be any) of having been acquainted with princes and other great persons arises from its being generally known to others; but never once mentioned by ourselves, if it can possibly be avoided. I say this perfectly for your service; because an universal opinion among those who know or have heard of you, that you have always practised a direct contrary proceeding, has done you more hurt than your natural understanding, left to itself, could ever have brought upon you. The world will never allow any man that character which he gives to himself by openly confessing it to those with whom he converses. Wit, learning, valour, great acquaintance, the esteem of good men will be known, although we should endeavour to conceal them, however they may pass unrewarded; but I doubt our own bare assertions upon any of those points will very little avail, except in tempting the hearers to judge directly contrary to what we advance. Therefore at this season of your life I should be glad you would act after the common custom of mankind, and have done with thoughts of Courts, of ladies, of lords, of politics, and all dreams of being important in the world. I am glad your country life has taught you Latin, of which you were altogether ignorant when I knew you first; and I am astonished how you came to recover it. Your new friend Horace will teach you many lessons agreeable to what I have said, for which I could refer to a dozen passages in a few minutes. I should be glad to see the house wholly swept of these cobwebs; and that you would take an oath never to mention a prince or princess, a foreign or domestic lord, an intrigue of state or of love; but suit yourself to the climate and company where your prudence will be to pass the rest of your life. It is not a farthing matter to you what is doing in Europe more than to every alderman who reads the news in a coffee-house. If you could resolve to act thus, your understanding is good enough to qualify you for any conversation in this Kingdom. Families will receive you without fear or restraint; nor watch to hear you talk in the grand style, laugh when you are gone, and tell it to all their acquaintance. It is a happiness that this quality may by a man of sense be as easily shaken off as it is acquired, especially when he has no proper claim to it; for you were not bred to be a man of business; you never were called to any employments at Courts; but destined to be a private gentleman, to entertain yourself with country business and country acquaintance; or, at best, with books of amusement in your own language. It is an uncontrolled truth that no man ever made an ill figure who understood his own talents, nor a good one who mistook them.

I am &c.

Jon. Swift.

There is a difficulty about the date of these two letters which I cannot clear up. The lameness from which Swift suffered, spoken of by Chetwode in his second letter, to which these are answers, is mentioned at least eight times in the Dean's published correspondence for 1732. On February 19th of that year, he wrote: "I have been above a fortnight confined by an accidental strain, and can neither ride nor walk, nor easily write." On March 13th Gay wrote to him: "I hope this unlucky accident of hurting your leg will not prevent your coming to us this spring." On May 4th he replied: "I am as lame as when you writ your letter." On June 30th he was able to ride "by virtue of certain implements called gambadoes, where my foot stands firm as on a floor." On July 10th he wrote to the Duchess of Queensberry: "Fortune has pleased, by one stumble on the stairs, to give me a lameness that six months have not been able perfectly to cure." On September 11th, in a letter to the Lord Mayor Elect, Alderman Barber, he said: "Nothing but this cruel accident of a lameness could have hindered me from attending your ceremonial as a spectator." About the same time he wrote to a friend: "I have been tied by the leg (without being married) for ten months past by an unlucky strain." There is also another mention of the lameness.

That it was in 1732 that he was lame there can be no question, for, independently of the dates of all these letters, it was on October 30th [1] of that year, as the *Gentleman's Magazine* shows, that Barber was sworn Lord Mayor. We might easily assume that Swift in writing to Chetwode had made a mistake in the year, but it is strange that he should have made it twice—both on April 28th and May 8th. There is a further difficulty : Chetwode seems to imply in his second letter that he was writing on the day he was leaving town, March 12th. If that was the case, it was on a Friday in March that he saw the Dean going to take horse. According to Swift's own account it was in the first days of February that he was lamed. He must have recovered enough to walk at least as far as Chetwode's lodgings.

Chetwode's "one little essay in a desperate Cause" was taking part in a Jacobite conspiracy, mentioned in an earlier letter. The books he bought on his foreign travels, which are still to be seen in the library at Woodbrook, show that he was not indifferent to literature. Swift's taunt was perhaps without justification. That it was deeply felt is shown by the reply which Chetwode sent.

[1] Till the change of style in 1752 the Lord Mayor entered into office on October 29. In 1732 that day fell on a Sunday.

LVIII.

[Coppy of my Letter to Dr Swift, in answer to his of
May ye 8th, 1731, rec^d at Wodebrooke.]

S^R,—Upon my return fm [from] a visitt I found
y^{rs} of ye 8th.   The Principle (you say) I approve in
my nature, yt [that] no Person ever offended me,
against whom I did not find some opportunity to
make him repent it, wd be of very little signification, did not the offending Parties aid and assist
me.   Had not Whitshed by corruption taken a
serv^t [servant] out my service into his, I had
probably never suspected y^t serv^t [that servant]
capable of being corrupted.   But as I found he
designd him for a Judas to betray his master, and
would give but (basely) 40 pieces of silver, I
thought it justifyable to give one piece more, by
which I fixed Whitshed in a Lodging at Pall-Mall,
to be cured of a dirty distemper, and had acct^s
[accounts] every Pacquett of his progress in the
Cure ; and when he got abroad, of his applications
to preside in our Chancery, upon his Brazen merritt
in favor of his friend Wood's halfpence ; this
Brodrick the Chancellor told me pinched Whitshed
more than Scrogg's censure throwne into his coach, or
even the 2 letters to the Rt. Honourable ——, and
swore by God, 'twas the best stratagem imaginable,
and that he should love me for it as long as he lived.

Raymond, that uninformed lump of clay, did cruelly disoblige and offend me, which compelled me to bring upon the Tapis Nanny Neary [?] cum sociis, to come at the cause of his mad disorders, and when discovered he to keep me silent and in humour betrayed every body, and all he knew, saw, heard or believed.   I know no family so cautious as you say, but some weake people subject to first impressions, and who, tho' clad in Glass Doublets, will be throwing of stones.   The objection of great names and tytles is a threadbare pretext for abusing me.   I am extremely sensible how low, little and malicious a spirritt reigns amongst some Folks, and am as sensible how difficult it is to live and converse with that dificult and mutable creature Man ; and yet I've done enough in the two great scenes of my Life to convince such (who are not proofe against Conviction) that it is my way to act according to my Reason, without being driven to anything contrary to my Inclination.   I can easily bear to be laughed at, for what I am sure is right ; besides I've reason to value myself that a Person of Honour wd condescend to make me a subject of jest ; and then I have company for my Comfort ; for I could tell you another besides whom Honour has rendered ridiculous as well as me.   Here is a Riddle for you, but you have a key for it, but as matters are circumstanced between you and me you must take care to turne it dexterously, in a distinction of Honour in the Concrete, and Honour in the Abstract, a distinction I could not for my blood pass over, I meane my vanity to shew you I understand a little Logick, as well as Lattin and Divinity.

You are merry upon my late Amour, and allow that Woemen have not lost all their charms with *me*, who could find any in a *Sybell*. But if you could do for me as *Maro* did by Æneas, and bring Sybella Cumæa to conduct me to the golden Branch—

Non solus Cadenus, sed eris mihi magnus Apollo.

What essays I've made, and whether to the disadvantage of my Fortune I know better than any other man living can. Whether I've any meritt with the present Folks is not of one farthing signification to the World ; tho' I've heard frequently of a sett of Puppies, who, as you say, affect to believe the first to my Dishonour ; as to my being Employed, I may answer as Lady Ann did to Glocester in Shakspear's Richard ye 3rd, 'Tis permitted to all men to hope. I cannot help what you say that you can't imagine what people can propose by attempts against me, but the present attempt is to represent me *as poor*, yt [that] I may the more easily be rendered Ridiculous, as well-knowing yt the loss of an ounce of Creditt is the loss of a pound of Power—what you observe of great names &c., it has always been my opinion that Principibus placuisse viris non ultima laus est—and Horace, with whom my becoming acquainted seems so great a miracle to you, saies, Tamen me cum magnis vixisse invita fatebitur usque Invidia. Your accts in some of yr latest Letters to me, yt everybody has dropp'd you, yt you are out of favour, yt you are forgotten and the like, minds me of ye fav'rite of Augustus, who was so great a master in the Art of declining Envy. 'Tis I think verily (in Dr. Swift) the merriest affectation I ever mett, that *you* who were bred under Sir Wm. Temple, and have been much about Court, especially 4 last years of Queen Ann, shd not know how to behave in presence of Troilus, and other sublime Irish Quallity. What think you of the Countess of Kerry since her Tripp to France? As to many things which regard me, I think Reason furnishes meanes sufficient to confound some who refuse to believe unless they can comprehend, and yt they are unwilling to do, to my Advantage. I meet some who love themselves too much to love a Friend, and I've often thought whether this and some other conduct has not been designed to take me off the expectation of frdship [friendship].

I did say, as you write, yt I intend for England ;
I can't guess who the Devill succeeds superanuated
Manly in his Intelligencers place of writing everything into England ; but it has been writt yt I was
to be at Chester such a day—and a Person came to
take me up in his Coach, and writes me a letter
filled with kind severity for having disappointed
him in what I never promised. I rec^d [received] a
Letter along with yours from *Dull-man* the Parson,
intended I suppose more to disturb than please me,
wherein he saies he rec^d a letter ab^t [about] me
wherein his Correspondent tells him that I see, and
feele, and hear, imagine, suspect, penetrate, and
foresee everything so well yt a man would be
tempted to believe that every one of my Passions
was guided by a sort of Magick, peculiar to me I
think. I've read these very words, or something
very like them, somewhere wh [which] this Coxcomb
wd apply to me, but cannot for my blood recollect
where. He adds yt he heard me terribly fallen
upon, and attacked abt so many folks (who had
offended me) dying in so short a time.

I am

Yr humble serv^t

K. C.

The friendly correspondence which had spread
over so many years is thus brought to a close
with mocks and gibes.

INDEX

A

Abjuration oaths, 87
Acheson, Sir Arthur, 222, 243
Addison, Joseph, 17, 46, 49, 57, 83, 97, 116
Aitken, George A., 208
Alberoni, Cardinal, 80
Aldrich, Dean, 158
Anne, Queen, 1, 4, 5, 207–9, 250
Arbuthnot, John, M.D., 5, 27, 44, 74, 86, 186, 196, 203
Atterbury, Bishop, 48, 65, 131, 165
Augustine, St., 96

B

Bank, National, 107, 110
Barber, Alderman John, 180, 238, 255
Bargon, Archdeacon, 115
Baron, the, 19, 51
Bathurst, Earl, 55, 226
Beaumont, Joseph, 63, 79
Behave, 55
Bentham, Jeremy, 63
Berkeley, Bishop, 149, 156, 193–5
Berkeley, Earl of, 21, 142
Bernard, Francis, 142
Bettesworth, Sergeant, 112
Bingley, Lord, 60, 62
Bishops, Irish, 147
Blackstone, Sir William, 220
Bolingbroke, Viscount, attainted, 36; price of his pardon, 37; escapes to France, 40, 43, 49; Tories and Jacobites, 62; attacks Lord Oxford, 191, 246; Swift a hypocrite reversed, 13;– love of him, 48;—want of civility, 83; —return to England, 215
Bolingbroke, Lady, 108
Bolton, Archbishop, 20
Boswell, James, 81, 198, 236
Boulter, Primate, 47, 76, 98, 147, 182, 196, 210, 228
Bravery, 91
Brent, Mrs., 84
Bright, John, 76
Bristol, 17
Brodrick, Lord Chancellor, 257
Brooke, Parson, 216
Bucknill, Dr., 45
Building, 94, 115, 117, 174
Bunyan, John, 203
Burke, Edmund, 110, 149
Burnet, Bishop, 123, 124, 238
Burney, Miss (Madame D'Arblay), 183
Burns, Robert, 198
Bush, Secretary, 142
Bussy Rabutin, 114, 117
Butler, Brinsley, 2, 6
Butler, Theophilus, 6

C

Cadenus and Vanessa, 189–96
Canal, 54
Cadogan, Earl, 164

Caroline, Queen, 196, 215

Carriers, 149

Carteret, Lord (Earl Granville), 150, 152, 156, 162, 165, 167-9, 171, 181

Carteret, Lady, 200

Castle Durrow, Lord, 111, 242

Champagné, Mayor, 17, 51, 56, 61

Chester, 66

Chesterfield, Earl of, 126, 133, 158

Chetwood, Crewe, 12

Chetwood, Knightley, *Advice to a Young Lady*, 18; foreign tour, 69, 78; honorary satisfaction, 103, 130; information of passages in private life, 240, 249, 257; Jacobite, 80, 256; library, 65, 256; marrying a second time, 233, 241, 244; perfumed paper, 150, 155; petition, 130; prosecuted, 87, 90, 93, 128, 131-44; quarrel with Colonel —, 90; quarrel with Swift, 244, separation from his wife, 154, 156, 162, 166, 169; son, 154, 219; spirit above his fortunes, 85; suspicions, 71; Ventoso, 252; walk, 50

Chetwood, Mrs., 22, 50, 60, 65, 154, 156, 162, 166, 169, 230

Churchill, Charles, 98

Clergy, Irish, 146

Clogher, Bishop of, 141

Coghill, Marmaduke, LL.D., 137, 140

Cole of the Oaks, 71

Collins, Churton, 239

Considerable, 139

Cork, Bishop of, 141

Cowper, Lord Chancellor, 149

Craik, Sir Henry, K.C.B., 239

Cromwell, Oliver, 95, 125

Cromwell, Richard, 95

Curll, Edmund, 123

Cusack, —, 241

D

D'Avaux, Count, 108

Davise, —, 24

Defoe, Daniel, 75

Delany, Patrick, D.D., 73, 83, 101, 125, 175, 182-4

Delany, Mrs., 16, 18, 48, 55, 67, 73, 133, 156, 182, 186, 217, 229, 243, 246

Derry, Deanery of, 142

De Veil, Colonel, 39

Dingley, Mrs., 17, 46, 200

Directions to Servants, 38

Dobbs, —, 121

Domestick, 135

Donellan, Mrs., 67

Dorset, Duke of, 73

Drapier Letters, 150, 160, 162, 165-6, 175, 181, 224, 244

Drapier's Hill, 243

Dryden, John, 33

Dublin, booksellers, 205; described by Mrs. Delany, 186; duels, 92; hospitality, 229, 242; Mayor squabble, 76; mob, 17, 37, 98; "most disagreeable place in Europe," 212; wretched, 180, 186

Dun, Morris, 115

E

Edgeworth, Richard Lovell, 159

Edgeworth, Maria, 6

Edinburgh, 98

England, cheap living, 232, 235-6

Essay on the Fates of Clergymen, 157

Evelyn, John, 56, 134

F

Fielding, Henry, 236

Finch, Mrs., 83

Fleetwood, Charles, 39

Flood, Henry, 69

Footmen, 36, 38

Forbes, Lady Jane, 14
Forbes, —, 134
Ford, Charles, 40, 43, 48, 62, 205
Forster, Chief Baron, 179
Forster, John, 89, 123, 205, 239
Fownes, Sir William, 170
Foxcroft, —, 49
French clergy in Dublin, 106, 108
Friends, 137–8

G

Gay, John, 49, 104, 197, 204, 226, 255
George I., 3, 8, 17, 24, 59, 77, 95, 131, 180, 214
George II., 95, 109, 215
Germain, Lady Betty, 73
Gibbon, Edward, 161
Giffard, Mrs., 243
Godolphin, Earl of, 208
Goldsmith, Oliver, 149, 191
Gould, Jay, 111
Grafton, Duke of, 92
Graham, —, 174
Granard, Earl of, 17, 56
Grattan, Henry, 74
Grattan, John, 79
Grattan family, 69, 73
Graves, —, 19
Gregg, William, 52, 58
Gulliver's Travels, 176, 186, 198, 202–9, 214
Gwynne, F., 3

H

Habeas Corpus Act suspended, 60, 131
Hale, Chief Baron, 181
Halifax, Earl of, 83
Hamilton, Lord Archibald, 85, 87
Hamilton, Lady, 85, 87
Hamilton, Sir William and Lady, 87
Hamilton, Mr. and Mrs., 243

Handel, George Frederick, 198
Harcourt, Lord Chancellor, 76
Harding, —, 182
Harrison, —, 185
Hawkesworth, John, 113
Health, 173, 179, 242
Hearne, Thomas, 16, 17, 62, 77, 89, 98, 119, 148, 157
Henley, Anthony, 83
History of the Four Last Years of Queen Anne, 197, 204
Holt, Mrs., 72
Holyhead, 66, 216
Honest people, 77
Horace, 59, 244, 260
Houghton, —, 36
How, —, 77
Howard, Mrs. (Countess of Suffolk), 215

I

Ireland, air, 198, 200; dog-hole, 201; famines, 227; obscure nook, 114; politics, 211; want of money, 225, 228; oppressed by England, 75, 93, 131, 197, 227; scene of misery, 197; roads, 217; sociableness, 218; Whigs and Tories, 124
Irish nation, 75; knavery, 120, 178; character of one another, 146; politicians, 217

J

Jackman, —, 153, 230, 237
Jackson, Rev. Daniel, 74, 79, 83, 103
James II., 56
Jervas, Charles, 100, 104, 115
Johnson, Esther (Stella), 17, 84, 177, 192, 200, 213, 239
Johnson, Samuel, advice, 235; beat Osborne, 247; building, 117; Highland tour, 81; Mad-

den's verses, 147 ; marrying for money, 237 ; "one" Johnson, 198 ; putting away a wife, 167 ; servant, 58 ; Swift's affectation, 82 ; — as Dean, 26 ; — illness, 45 ; — marriage, 239 ; — letters, 133 ; —dread of hypocrisy, 13 ; —frugal of his wine, 16 ; Whigs, 16

Jonson, Ben, 22, 34
Jordan, —, 2, 34
Judges renewed, 26

K

Kelly, Miss, 183
Kendal, Duchess of, 151
Kennet, Bishop, 3
Kerry, Countess of, 260
Killala, Bishop of, 243
King, Archbishop, 4, 35, 36, 46, 48, 76, 87, 90, 92, 102, 130, 133, 147, 181, 203, 209, 217
King, —, 160
Kings, Divine right of, 89
Kneller, Sir Godfrey, 104

L

Landlords, Irish, 131
Lane-Poole, Stanley, 239
Langford, Sir Arthur, 86
Langton, Peregrine, 236
Laracor, 7, 27, 86
La Touche, J. J. Digges, LL.D., 140
Law, study of, 219
Le Brunt, —, 122
Legion Club, 68
Letter to a Young Clergyman, 219
Letters from Nobody, 166
Leving, Chief Justice, 144, 148
Lewis, Erasmus, 38, 76
Life, last act a tragedy, 214
Lightburne, Rev. Stafford, 174, 179
London, Bishop of (John Robinson), 51, 55

London, Lord Mayor of, 16, 97, 181, 256
London, tumults, 51
London to Dublin, 199, 216
Londonderry Society, 148
Longford, Earl of, 178
Lords, Irish, 69, 81

M

Mackintosh, Sir James, 74
Madden, Samuel, D.D., 8, 147, 158
Madhouses, 171
Magee, Alexander, 125
Magistrates, 23
Mankind, 106, 109, 133, 185, 241
Manley, Isaac, 19, 20, 36, 43
Mar, Earl of, 62
Marishy, 54
Marlborough, Duke of, 16, 164
Marlborough, second Duke of, 56
Marrying for money, 237
Marseilles, Bishop of, 118
Marshall, Robert, 193
Mason, Rev. William, 183
Mason, W. Monck, 239
Milton, John, 66, 197
Mist's Journal, 94
Mob, 55
Molière, 87
Montagu, Lady Mary Wortley, 8, 62, 68, 204
Montaigne, 198
Morphew, —, 124
Motte, Benjamin, 75, 195, 205-7 209

N

Naboth's Vineyard, 145, 179
Nelson, Viscount, 87
Newcastle, Holles, Duke of, 246
Newcastle, Pelham, Duke of, 140, 166, 168
Newton, Sir Isaac, 151

Nichols, John, 55
Northumberland, Duchess of, 184

O

"One" Mr. R. Walpole, 197
Orleans, Duke of, 80
Ormond, Duke of, fled to France, 37, 59, 61 ; reward offered, 38 ; huzzaed, 40, 62 ; impeached, 41, 43, 48–9 ; invasion of Scotland, 80 ; snuff, 50 ; Swift's friend, 83
Ormond, Duchess of, 6, 37
Orrery, Earl of, 182
Osborne, Thomas, 247
Owen, Ellen, 12
Oxford, Robert Harley, Earl of, Bolingbroke's enmity, 191 ; death, 144, 148 ; dragon, 74 ; hissed and cheered, 40 ; impeached, 36, 48–9, 57 ; imprisoned, 58, 64, 70 ; intrepidity, 52 ; Lord Treasurer, 4 ; plague, 118 ; refuses to flee, 61 ; son's marriage, 246 ; Swift's compliment, 72 ; *vive la bagatelle*, 102
Oxford, second Earl of, 246
Oxford, Countess of, 246
Oxford University, 155–7, 161
Oxford town, 17, 62

P

Pall Mall Coffee-house, 73
Panting, Matthew, D.D., 77
Park Gate, 67
Parliament, Irish, 68, 72, 138
Parnell, Thomas, 66
Parvisol, Joseph, 85
Pendarves, Mrs., *see* Delany
Pepys, Samuel, 238
Percival, —, 85
Percy, Bishop, 184
Pilkington, Rev. Matthew, 207
Pilkington, Mrs., 126, 145

Plague, 115, 118, 121
Pope, Alexander, Bishop Berkeley, 194–5 ; *Epistle to Jervas*, 104 ; fortune increased, 233 ; *Gulliver's Travels*, 204 ; *Homer*, 4 ; Ireland, 116 ; letters, 133 ; Marseilles' bishop, 118 ; servant, 127 ; Swift visits him, 191, 212 ; Swift and Walpole, 197 ; university lads' admiration of him, 220 ; wine, 16
Post-office, post days, 8 ; post horses, 6 ; letters opened, 20, 35 ; post from England, 73
Pratt, Benjamin, D.D., 72, 106, 108
Preaching, limitation on, 24, 27
Pretender, 8, 10, 17, 37–8, 48, 59, 71, 76, 97, 130
Prior, Matthew, 52, 57, 102, 197
Prisons, 47, 96
Projectors, 63
Proposal for the Universal Use of Irish Manufacture, 131

Q

Queensberry, Duchess of, 82, 255
Quilca, 175

R

Rabble, 55
Ramicus, 118
Ramsay, Allan, 194
Raymond, Rev. Dr., 41, 44
Reformer, 121
Restoration, 95
Reynolds, Sir Joshua, 58
Reynolds, Miss, 58
Richardson, Samuel, 205
Rochfort, George, 50, 101–3
Rogers, Thomas, 119
Roses, white, 94, 97
Rowe, Nicholas, 34
Rowley, —, 107
Russell, Dr., 159

S

Sale, —, 185

Sandis, —, 91

Scarborough, Earl of, 204

Scott, Sir Walter, 6, 33, 55, 73, 113, 239

Secret Committee, 42, 48

Secretaries of the Lord-Lieutenant, 142

Servants, 11, 52, 122, 125

Shakespeare, William, 31, 33

Sheldon, Archbishop, 237

Sheridan, Thomas, D.D., 83, 121, 141, 175, 177, 194

Shirley, —, 231

Shrewsbury, Duke of, 52, 57, 60

Shrewsbury, Duchess of, 82

Smollett, Tobias, 27, 36, 169

Somers, Lord, 57, 83

Spain, war with, 81

Squires, Irish, 81, 117

St. Ambrose, 245

St. Patrick's Cathedral, chapter dinner, 221, 223; choir, 2, 4, 29; deanery house and garden, 7, 9, 10, 107, 129; elms, 107, 113; endowments, 23; liberty, 4, 107, 111; visitation, 23, 26

Steele, Sir Richard, 83

Stella, *see* Johnson, Esther

Stephen, Leslie, 239

Sterne, Bishop, 13, 15

Sterne, Laurence, 149

Stopford, James, D.D., 145, 149, 153, 156, 159, 169–71, 174, 180, 232, 234

Sunderland, Earl of, 51, 56

Swift, Deane, 31, 55, 112, 239

Swift, Jonathan, ambition cured, 250; butler, 112; card-playing, 172; civility, 83; clothes and washing, 6; coffee, 20, 21; Court life, 3, 196, 211; deafness, 45, 105, 116, 121, 155, 212; dean, a smart, 24; "the Dean," 37;

defends his rights, 4, 210; described by Mrs. Delany, 183; Dublin common people, 37, 200, 224; England, love of, 190, 197, 201, 214; exercise, 187; exile in Ireland, 117; eye-sight, 176; faithful friend, 58, 64; familiarity with the great, 82; fears the worst, 217; fond of pranks, 73; French, 88, 106; friends with people of his own level, 85, 249; funeral, 125; giddiness, 45, 213; gold watch, 3; grandmother's proverbs, 31–2; hates mankind, 109, 133, 186, 241; health, labours for, 242; home comforts, 213, 217, 242; horses, 2, 5, 94; housekeeper, 84, 112; improvements, 89, 173, 185; income, 9, 10; lame, 247, 255; law-suit, 226, 230; letters to Pope, 133; letters destroyed, 183; libelled, 221, 224, 241; library, 9, 12, 34; marriage reported, 238; *Miscellanies*, 121, 123; money, want of ready, 7, 225; monkish life, 202, 212; nervous about infectious disorders, 118; news, ignorant of, 28, 30, 122, 175, 180; plate, 230; politicks forsworn, 79, 83, 129; prayers, 12; preferments, 143; proclamation against him, 150, 175, 181; puddings, 242; riding, 187, 245; servant dies, 125; — discharged, 126; — board wages, 229; — livery, 230; shaving, 31; snuff, 50, 52; stir in London about him, 190, 196; suspected Jacobite, 35–7, 41, 48, 68, 72, 77; titled people shunned, 79, 212, 217, 249; trusted, expected to be, 72; *vive la bagatelle*, 45, 102; weather and health, 45; Whig in politics, 16, 89; wine, 15, 46, writings, anonymous, 123; — fathered on him, 121, 123; — for money, 204

T

Taylor, John, D.D., 117
Temple, Sir William, 89, 135, 204, 243, 260
Thackeray, William Makepeace, 159, 164
Thorold, —, 3
Tickell, Thomas, 195
Tillotson, Archbishop, 146
Took, Rev. Mr., 206, 209
Tooke, Benjamin, 70, 75, 124
Tories, 59, 62
Townshend, Viscount, 165
Trim, 26
Trinity College, Dublin, 42, 46–8, 51, 157–61, 220

U

Universities, 219
Usher, Archbishop, 158
Usher, Mrs., 243

V

Vanhomrigh, Esther, 101, 176, 189–96
Ventoso, 80, 252

W

Wales, Frederick Prince of, 87
Wall, —, 90
Wallace, Sir William, 197
Waller, Edmund, 145
Walls, Archdeacon, 19, 50, 53, 187
Walpole, Horatio (Lord Walpole), 167, 169
Walpole, Horace (Earl of Orford), 102
Walpole, Sir Robert (Earl of Orford), 62, 165, 196, 214, 246
Walpole, Lady, 215
Warburton, Rev. Thomas, 59, 61
Webb, —, 240
Wellington, Duke of, 26
Wesley, Rev. John, 97
Wesley, —, 86
Wharton, Marquis of, 20–2
Wharton, Duke of, 22
Whigs, 16, 121, 124
Whiteway, Mrs., 125, 204
Whitshead, Chief Justice, 129, 132, 257
Wightman, General, 81
William III., 46, 48, 56, 146
Windsor Prophecy, 54
Wine, price of, 16
Wood, William, 150, 160, 162, 165
Wycherly, William, 34, 247

Y

Young, Arthur, 90, 117, 178, 218, 236

The Gresham Press

UNWIN BROTHERS,

WOKING AND LONDON.

www.ingramcontent.com/pod-product-compliance
Lightning Source LLC
Chambersburg PA
CBHW060520030726
47498CB00004B/1012